WORKING TOGETHER

Working Together

Paul's Letter to the
Philippians for Today's Church

Pandang Yamsat

AFRICA CHRISTIAN TEXTBOOKS

2018

Working Together
Paul's Letter to the Philippians for Today's Church
Copyright © 2018 Pandang Yamsat

Africa Christian Textbooks (ACTS)

ACTS Bookshop, International HQ, TCNN,
PMB 2020, Bukuru, Plateau State, 930008, Nigeria
GSM: +234 (0) 803-589-5328; E-mail: pa@actsnigeria.org
Website: http://actsnigeria.org

ISBN: 9789789054114 Print
ISBN: 9789789054121 ePub
ISBN: 9789789054138 Mobi

Cover Design: Billy Abwa
Book Design: Peter Fleck

DEDICATION

My wife, Magdalene Yamsat
in commemoration of our 42 years of happy and blessed marriage

CONTENTS

FOREWORD

As you travel round many Nigerian cities, you are bound to encounter billboards advertising a religious crusade. Nigerians after all, have a well-deserved reputation for being among the most religious people on earth! Often these billboards will have some variation of the following text:

Come and See the Man of God. Come and Get Your Miracle!

Yet in so doing we actually put these preachers on pedestals, thinking they are somehow infallible, and in reality, our attitude towards them, and sometimes towards other Christian ministers, is little short of idolatry.

Professor Yamsat has, thus done the church in Nigeria a service by highlighting how the Apostle Paul, despite being one of the greatest evangelists there ever was, stressed the theme of partnership in his Letter to the Philippians. Paul did not seek to exalt his own position – indeed, he reckoned all of his earthly qualifications to be rubbish when compared with knowing Jesus. Instead, he worked as part of an evangelistic team. Here in Philippians he mentions Timothy and Epaphroditus. Elsewhere in his letters and in Acts, we encounter Mark, Silas, Priscilla & Aquilla, and Apollos to mention a few. Working together, however, did not just include the full time evangelistic team that worked with Paul. It also included the churches that Paul had started, and especially in this case the Philippian church. Through their prayerful and practical support they supported Paul spiritually and financially and he saw them as just as much a part of his team as the evangelists with whom he worked every day. Without their committed support, neither Paul nor any of his evangelist colleagues could have achieved the success they enjoyed. Yet working together also involves sharing in suffering. Paul writes from a Roman prison where he faces the very real possibility of execution. Their working together in the gospel was not a matter of sharing out wealth and political power but of patient endurance and service so that Christ's Name would be glorified and his kingdom extended.

Another theme that Professor Yamsat brings out is that when the Philippians became believers they entered into a Christian citizenship. As such, their loyalties and conduct was different to those of the Roman citizens and others around them. This distinctive lifestyle, conduct and message naturally brought them into conflict with the cultural, religious and political systems of the day – another reason for the sharing as partners with Paul in suffering.

Yet in all of this suffering, Paul enjoins his readers to rejoice, to praise God for what He is doing in and through them, and to press on towards the goal that Christ has for them: the prize of everlasting glory in heaven with Christ.

Surely, in all of these themes there is a message for Christians in Nigeria today?

Dr Paul Todd
ACTS HQ, Bukuru,
May 2018

PREFACE

The Letter to the Philippians has received a lot of attention from scholars and Christians generally, most especially because of its personal and friendly content, even though someone who was in chains in a Roman prison writes it.

This exposition reflects, not only many years of teaching Philippians to students at different levels, but also more recently my three months' post-graduate studies at Wheaton College, Wheaton, Illinois, USA in 2013. There I enjoyed the help and guidance of Prof. Lynn H. Cohick, to whom I am very grateful for the support given me during that time. This study was made possible by a grant from Langham Partnership International for which I am also very grateful. As a Langham Scholar, this added support for my academic and spiritual growth makes my appreciation of Langham Partnership International far more than tongue can tell. I appreciate Ian Shaw, and Fred Gale of Langham Partnership for encouraging me while at Wheaton College during my post-doctoral studies on this work. I also thank Jeffrey Greenman, Ann Gerber and Daniel Block of Wheaton College and an African friend I met at Wheaton.

This exposition is not simply an academic pursuit but a spiritual one, drawing lessons for the persecuted church of today from what was of great importance in the mutual relationship between Paul and the church in Philippi during their times of external and internal crises in the first century. This exposition is, therefore, intended to help students of theology and church leaders and members to come to grip with this ancient but all-important letter in uniting the church to forge ahead steadfastly to its anticipated salvation in spite of whatever crises the church may have in her hands.

I am grateful to my Master of Theology class for helping me to have deeper insight into this letter prior to going into print. They helped me to appreciate the practicality of this letter in the life of a persecuted church in our era and the need to remain steadfast and one in its struggle to be the true church of God.

Being apart from my wife, Magdalene, for three months was not easy for her, but she endured it, for which I am grateful and thus I dedicate the book to her.

I appreciate Mrs. Alice John Mawu, my secretary who typed in the corrections and my daughter Gambeer R. Gutip who checked the final script for any grammatical and typing errors. However, any errors found in this book cannot be attributed to her but are mine to bear.

Above all, I am grateful to the late Professor Je'adayibe D. Gwamna and Dr. Paul Todd for taking their valuable time to edit this work and to Paul Todd for writing the Foreword.

INTRODUCTION

First century letters

There are different types of ancient letters, including, private, official, literary, recommendation, treaties, philosophical, and fictional, as well as those of the New Testament. Such letters were all similar in form. The purpose of the letter is also the same. They were a means of communication and interaction in writing to compensate for the absence of face-to-face contact and interaction created by distance. Because of this, such letters carried with them the rhetoric that would have been part-and-parcel of a face-to-face interaction on the letter's subject matter. Aune rightly observes that by the first century BC, rhetoric had already influenced letter writing. By that time, it had become both as a means of communication as well as a "sophisticated instrument of persuasion and media," used especially by the educated in their interaction with one another or others outside their reach. This followed a certain course of action.[1] Paul's letters, including Philippians, belong to such letters.

---

[1] David E. Aune, *The New Testament in Literary Environment*, Philadelphia, 1987. p. 160.

Typically, a letter was known to be a letter by its format, which carried the name of the addressor or author with his title or status and that of the recipient(s) at the beginning of the letter called, "the Address."

The Address is followed with a salutation, usually, using simply one word, "greetings" followed by an inquiry concerning the health of the recipient as well as informing the recipient of the author's healthy state, as we find in Nigerian traditional letters. In most cases, this is followed by a thanksgiving to the gods for some good deeds done to the author(s) by the gods or done by the recipient(s) or some other persons. A transitional formula is used to transit from the thanksgiving to the main purpose of the letter, the body of the letter, which could cover several issues joined together by transitional formulae or it could simply have only one issue to relate to the recipient(s). The letter closes with a network of greetings from the author(s). The author also passes on the greetings of those with him to the recipients who, in turn, are asked to pass on his greetings to their contacts. That these greetings are found in almost all ancient letters shows the significance of greetings in ancient letters and confirms the fact that letters were important in building bridges across distances. Lastly, the greetings were followed by the one word, "Farewell."

An example of such letters may help give a feeling of Greco-Roman letters:

> Apion to Epimachos, his father and lord, very many greetings.
>
> Before all else I pray that you are well and that you may prosper in continual health, together with my sister and her daughter and my brother.
>
> I give thanks to the lord Serapis, because when I was endangered at sea, he rescued (me) immediately.

When I arrived at Misenium, I received as traveling money (uiaticum) from Caesar three gold pieces, and I am well.

Therefore I request you, my lord father, write me a letter, first about your welfare, secondly about the welfare of my siblings, thirdly, in order that I may make obeisance before your hand(writing), because you trained me well, and I hope by this means quickly to advance, the gods willing.

Salute Kapiton very much and my siblings and Serenilla and my friends. I send my portrait to you through Euktemonos. My name is Antonius Maximus.

I pray you are well.

Company Anthenonike.

Serenos the son of Agathodaimon, salute you ... and ... the (son) of ....ros, and Tourbon, the son of Gallonios, and D ... nas, the (son) of ... (found on the left margin as addendum).[2]

This letter is similar to traditional Nigerian letters, which normally give the name of the author and recipient at the beginning and ask for the well-being or health of the recipient as well as share with the recipient the condition of health of the letter writer, like:

From Mr. David Naanfwang to Mr. John Izang

After thousands of greetings, I want to let you know that .....

---

[2]BGU II 423 (dated 2nd Century CE) and translated by J. L. White, *Ancient Letters* 1986, p. 10.

Greet Mama Maryamu John for me and her children.

Grace and peace be with you.

From me Teacher Istifanus Pam

The greetings are never taken lightly. They are as important as the body of the letter, if not more, because they serve as a substitute for the absence of face-to-face contact and interaction.

When we look at Paul's letters and other New Testament letters, we observe that they follow the same general outline of ancient letters. However, in all of these letters, we find that Paul gives each a more elaborate and theological face than we find in typical Greco-Roman letters. In other words, although Paul followed the ancient letter format from opening to closing, greeting and farewell, he was free enough not to slavishly follow the convention of his time, in order to meet his need and that of his recipient(s). He gave the opening greeting and thanksgiving a Christian touch, as well as the closing greeting and benediction,[3] For example, in Philippians, Paul writes:

Philippians

Address
[1]Paul and Timothy, who are slaves of Jesus Christ, to all the saints in Christ Jesus who are in Philippi, together with the bishops and deacons.

Salutation
[2]Grace to you and peace from God our Father and our Lord Jesus Christ.

---

[3]John L. White 1986, p. 29.

Thanksgiving and prayer

I give thanks to my God concerning you every time I remember you. [4]Always in all my prayers for all of you, I do pray with joy, [5]because of your partnership in the gospel from the first day until now. [6]Confident of the fact that he who began this good work in you will bring it to completion until the appointed time of Jesus Christ. [7]As it is right of me to think this [way] about all of you, because I have you in my heart. Also in my imprisonment and in the defence and confirmation of the gospel, all of you were my fellow-partners in the grace [of God]. [8]For God is my witness, how I long for all of you with the innermost affection of Christ Jesus.

Letter Body 1: 12 - 4: 20

I want you to know that …

Closing Greeting and Benediction, 4: 21 - 23

[21]Greet all the saints in Christ Jesus. The brethren with me do greet you. [22]All the saints greet you, especially those from the house of Caesar.

[23]The grace of the Lord Jesus Christ be with your spirit.

Authorship, occasion and purpose

There is much in this letter to inform us about its authors. The letter does not leave us in doubt about either the authors, or the occasion and purpose for its writing. The opening of the letter tells us Paul and Timothy are co-authors of the letter. While scholars generally agree that Paul is the author of the letter to the Philippians, they wonder, however, why the content of the letter does not reflect Timothy as co-author with Paul in the content of the letter as well as in the address. However, this question arises because we are thinking in today's context where everyone wants acknowledgement of his or her involvement fearing the facelessness of anonymity.

Only a very few scholars disagree with Paul's authorship of the letter because they believe that chapters 3 and 4 are out of tune with the rest of the letter. Examples of such scholars are F. C. Baur, who rejects Pauline authorship completely, and Helmut Koester who disagrees with Paul's authorship, but says that it is a compilation of three letters of Paul, written at three different times and compiled by a later editor.[4] However, as has been said, these views owe more to a lack of close attention to the epistolary and rhetorical style and structure of Paul's letters. Such scholars, who fail to see the interrelatedness of this letter, should note that Paul is not a novice in the rules of letter and speech writing or oratory. Paul was by training a scholar of note, an orator, writer and pastor and missionary and so he had a wide knowledge of what was going on in his time, including business, being a tent maker. Not only was Paul a good scholar and writer but he was by far a very innovative scholar, as his letters testify.

However, since it is certain Paul used amanuenses or scribes to write his letters, it is possible that they could have influenced the way his letters are written. Even then, whether the letter was dictated to the scribes or the scribes wrote it under his overall direction, it would still be read to him before he put his signature to it and dispatched the letter. By so doing, he could still shape it to his liking.

What, therefore, do we gather from the letter to the Philippians about the person of Paul that adds to our understanding? Paul is portrayed as a devoted spiritual leader, preacher, missionary and writer who was conversant with the styles of letter writing of his day. He is willing and able to adjust the letter conventions of his day to suit his

---

[4]"Letter to the Philippians" in *Interpreter's Dictionary of the Bible: Supplementary Volume*, Ed. K. Crimet all. (Nashville: Abingdon, 1976), p. 665).

Christian context, rather than allow the conventions to dictate how he should write. Today, we allow societal norm to dictate how we do things in church. Paul longed for the conversion of unbelievers into the Christian faith and for the growth and unity of the church of God, especially those churches he founded. A study of his other letters, for example, First Corinthians, shows his desire for the unity of the church of God, irrespective of social, spiritual or academic status, race and tribe. This is because his ecclesiology is tied to his Christology. Before Christ went back to heaven, he prayed to God the Father for the unity of the church he founded. This prayer for unity was based on the grounds that just as he and the Father are one, so believers too must be one and indwelt by God "so that the world may believe that you sent me" (John. 17: 20 - 23). Paul took this prayer for unity so seriously that Gentiles and Jews were to worship together in all the churches he founded, and he sought to unite these Gentile churches with the Jerusalem church (Acts 15). He did this through encouraging the Gentile churches to demonstrate this unity by financially supporting the famine-stricken church in Jerusalem (1 Corinthians 16: 1 - 4; 2 Cor. 8 and 9). Paul, therefore, emulated the Lord Jesus by not being racist, tribalist or a status conscious person (Phil. 2: 5ff).

Paul was very aware of the politics of his day and the Roman law that guaranteed certain rights and privileges to its citizens. He not only knew these rights but also used them for the purposes of spreading the gospel across the Roman Empire. Yet, as much as Paul respected those laws and used them to the advance of the gospel, he was not a slave to those laws. In fact, as will be seen in this letter, he used the same titles *kurios/* "lord", *soteria/* "saviour" that were normally reserved for the emperor and sometimes his generals. Instead, he ascribed them to Jesus Christ, for which ascription he was liable to be charged with treason or insurrection. Despite the seriousness of the matter, Paul was not executed in Thessalonica (Acts 17). He also used terms like *politeuma/* "citizen" or the verb *politueein* ("to live as citizen") to refer to the believing community in Philippi and the manner in which they were to conduct themselves in accordance with the gospel of Jesus Christ; a manner quite in contrast to the way the citizens of Rome or Philippi conducted themselves. Paul was thus more than a free man. He defended and protected the freedom of the gospel and the church. He was free to express the gospel the way he felt it right, so as to take the gospel and church far and near in the best way he could, without fear or favour, alive or dead, chained in prison or out of prison, for the same cause. The furtherance of the gospel and the progress of the gospel and salvation of believers everywhere were of more value to him than his own personal life and safety or comfort. Thus, he adopted a theology that stated that the authorities could not stop the gospel from moving from one place to another. Since the gospel was more important than his food, his life and his security, the Roman government could not stop him. If he was imprisoned, the gospel would find a foothold there in prison and his fellow preachers outside the prison would be encouraged to preach the gospel more than ever before, because of the example that Paul's faith and courage set before them (Acts 16; Phil. 1: 12 - 14). Believers were strengthened by his faith and encouraged to hear that even in prison people were won for Christ by his witness there. It mattered not for Paul if he were killed for the sake of the gospel, because to be killed meant rest with Christ from his labours (Phil. 1: 12 - 26) while to live meant progress for the gospel. Thus, either way he was no loser, for Paul knew and experienced the saving grace and work of God in Jesus Christ. This same Jesus, who, even though he was divine, had humbled himself and become a human being, identifying with even the worst of all people, through death on the cross in order to save men and women. Then he had triumphed over death by rising from the dead to be seated beside the Father in the heavens. For Paul, therefore, no amount of intimidation by the authorities could restrict or chain the gospel from spreading everywhere.

Paul was also a good leader, giving credit to Timothy and Epaphroditus, whom today we would call juniors, in the work of the gospel. In this letter, he mentions Timothy as his co-author lavishing praise on him, and also commending Epaphroditus to the Philippians. He does the same in his other letters concerning Timothy. He recognizes them as partners, working together in the gospel, valuing their contribution to the growth of the church and to enriching his own spiritual and material needs. Thus, for Paul, no one is so exalted spiritually and materially as to look down on any fellow believer, or to refuse to receive from any believer(s) (Phil. 3: 12 - 14; 4: 10 - 20). Paul's only concern on receiving gifts was if the gift would reduce his freedom to preach the gospel as he should, as was the case with the Corinthians' gift that he could not accept (I Cor. 9: 15; 2 Cor. 11: 7 - 12). For him, whether high or low in the church's hierarchy, leaders or members, all work together in the gospel, with each having his or her contribution to make for the growth of the church and the gospel, according to the gift given (Phil. 1; 1 - 11, 4: 10 - 20; Cor. 12-14; Eph. 4: 1 - 16; Rom. 12: 3 - 8). The positions we each occupy in the church of God therefore entail responsibilities and are not for feasting or lording it over those below. Like Jesus, for Paul, he who would want to be great, must be the one who humbles himself and serves others (Phil. 2: 5 - 11; Luke. 9: 46 - 48; John. 13: 12 - 15).

And as the most prolific writer of all the apostles, Paul was not only a good letter writer like his contemporaries outside the church (e.g. Seneca), but a good innovator in the writing industry of his time. As much as he was conventional in his letter-writing technique, he was so innovative that he created for Christendom its own way of letter writing. Paul was very much a free preacher and leader who could freely use the conventions of his time as long as they served his gospel purpose. Nevertheless, he also felt free to reform the conventions of his day to suit his Christian purpose. He wrote intimate and friendly letters to the churches he founded, as in the Letter to the Philippians. His letters are open, frank and brotherly, like that to the Corinthians and a letter of rebuke, like that to the Galatians, for example. He normally began with a frank introduction giving thanks for the good that was noticed in the recipients, or getting straight to the point when nothing good could be said, as in the Galatian letter. Paul was true to his thanksgiving about the audience, because his confidence rested, not in himself and his ability and wisdom to make the audience or congregation listen to him, but his confidence was in the one who had called him into the preaching of the gospel. That is why, even though he was proposing to the Philippians that they live their lives only as citizens of the gospel and of heaven in the midst of oppositions by opponents; even though this was likely to be interpreted as treason, he still pressed on them to so live, because he believed therein was their salvation.

The letter also tells us the occasion in which Paul wrote to the Philippian church. In 1: 7, 12 - 10, we understand he was writing at a time he was in prison. From his mention of the Praetorian Guard, it appears that he was in Rome, but see below for discussion about when he wrote. He wrote at a time when he was in great need and the Philippians were feeling for him to the extent that they sent Epaphroditus to him along with a gift (1: 5; 4: 10 - 20). The letter also tells us that he was writing at a time that the Philippians were in high spirits about living their faith in love for one another (1: 9) even though they were being confronted by enemies from without (1: 27 -

30) and enemies from within the church (3: 3, 18-19). He also wrote when Euodia and Syntyche, two leaders in the church, were not getting along, prompting him to call them to order and into reconciliation (4: 2 - 3).

These happenings in the church show what Paul's purpose was in writing to the church. As he had founded the church, and now worked very closely with it in his evangelistic work, he needed to raise a number of issues with them. From the letter, especially, 1: 3 - 7, 27 - 30 and 4: 10 - 20, Paul writes the Philippian Christians in order to:

1. Share with them his prayerful gratitude to God for their partnership with him in preaching the gospel, in cash and kind and to let them know of his constant prayer that God would make their love increase with knowledge and discernment (1: 3 - 11; 4: 10 - 20);

2. Thank the Philippian Church for their gift of money and for sending Epaphroditus to aid him in his imprisonment (4: 10 - 20). He wants to show them that what ultimately matters is not so much the gift that makes him appreciate their kind gesture but that their accounts in heaven have been credited to them as a result;

3. Encourage them to strive and persevere in the face of persecution from opponents outside the church and false teaching and preaching from within the church (1: 27 - 30; 3: 3, 8 - 9; 4: 5), emulating his own example (1: 12 - 26; 2: 17 - 18);

4. Encourage the church to live in unity by having the same attitudes and to live in harmony with one another sincerely taking to heart the interests of one another. To do that, they should not shy away from reconciling any warring personalities within the church. As believers in Jesus Christ, they should be considerate of the interests of one another and not each sticking to his or her

personal interests. As followers of Christ, unity, humility and self-sacrifice should be their watchword, in the same way as Jesus did while here on earth (1: 27 - 2: 18; 4: 2 - 3).

As has been said, we know from the Philippian letter that Paul is writing from prison (Phil. 1: 7, 13, 14, 16), an imprisonment, which he says could result either in death or release (1: 20 - 26; 2: 17). However, the letter does not say when or where this happened, and we have no mention of it anywhere else. Acts tells us of three imprisonments of Paul, the Philippian imprisonment in Acts 16: 16 - 40 in about 51/52 AD, the Caesarean imprisonment in Acts 21: 32 - 23: 30, about AD 57-59 and the Roman imprisonment or better, house arrest in Acts 28: 30f, about AD 61/62. Others talk of a fourth imprisonment in Ephesus, around AD 53-55, even though it is not mentioned anywhere that he was imprisoned there, but because of the mention of Praetorian Guards in Ephesus.

For this reason, the date for writing the letter largely depends on which imprisonment Paul was referring to when he was writing the Letter to the Philippians. If it was during Paul's imprisonment in Philippi when he was imprisoned for healing a demon-possessed slave girl who foretold the future, during his second missionary journey, the date of writing would be AD 51 (Acts 16: 6 - 40). However, this is unlikely because he was in the prison for only a few days and the content of the letter does not suggest he wrote to the church in those few days. Nor would he have written when he was in the same city with them. A later date is therefore more likely. The suggestion of a date between AD 53 and 55 at Ephesus is not feasible because there is no mention of Paul's imprisonment in Ephesus, even though there was a *praetorium* in Ephesus. Nor can Caesarea be the place of writing, even though there was an army regiment there. This is because there was not much freedom for Paul to write the way he writes in this letter during that imprisonment. His hope to be out of prison was not possible because of the level of corruption relating to that imprisonment (cf. Acts 23:31 – 25:32). It was for that reason that Paul appealed to Caesar in Rome. The letter therefore could not have been written at Caesarea in about 57-59 but later. The remaining imprisonment we know of is in Rome, after his long imprisonment in Caesarea. The Roman imprisonment is therefore the most feasible place of writing this letter, probably about 61 AD reflecting the considerable freedom he had in that imprisonment, with opportunities to do what he wanted to do and for visitors to visit and even stay with him. It is this is the kind of prison scene that we read of in both thee Philippian letter and in Acts 28.

The city, its people and the Church

Philippi was a well-known city before and at the time of Paul. It was a commercial centre and a Roman colony and therefore its inhabitants had the privileges of being Roman citizens and thus free from taxation.

The history of Philippi goes well back to 356 BC. In 356, Philip II, the king of Macedon, father of Alexander the Great, took over the gold area of Pangaeus by subduing the Thracian region, to which Pangaeus belonged. Thereafter, Philip established the city of Philippi after his own name.[5] He fortified Philippi and established a strong military base in the city to guard his gold mines. This was a strategic move by the king as the city provided security as well as good communications to both the west and the east for the sale of the gold and other commodities. After the Romans defeated the Macedonians in the

---

[5]Peter O'Brien, *The Epistle to the Philippians*.3; Hansen, G.. Walter, *The Letter to the Philippians,* 1-2; David Stockton, "The Founding of the Empire" in *The Oxford History of the Classical World*, Ed. John Boardman, Jasper Griffin and Oswyn Murray, London, Oxford Univ. Press, 1988. pp. 531-556.

battle of 168-167 BC, Philippi became one of the four districts of Macedonia in the Roman Empire. Then in 42 BC, it was made a Roman colony after Mark Anthony and Octavian defeated Brutus and Cassius, the assassins of Julius Caesar, the Emperor. Many of their veteran soldiers were settled in Philippi.[6] As a result, everything of Philippi became Roman, the people's life and dress, the laws governing the city, the city's language and the rights and privileges of the people. They had the same rights and privileges as the Romans living in Rome. Eventually Octavian defeated Anthony, became the Emperor and took on the name Augustus. He sent more veterans to Philippi, especially Anthony's loyalists. Philippi became a little Rome; governed by Roman law from then on right to the time Paul came into the city and founded a church there, the first church on European soil, in 51/52 AD. Yet, although Philippi became a Roman colony with the rights of citizenship of Rome, only a small percentage of the inhabitants enjoyed such citizenship. Far from being granted citizenship, the locals were deprived of their farmlands in order to settle these citizens who came from Rome or elsewhere. Numbers of Roman citizens were thus restricted, thereby ensuring the Romans socio-economic status:

> Citizenship carried with it the right to hold political office and responsibility in the Roman state. It gave the right to participate in the deliberations of Roman assemblies. It gave the right to inherit Roman property and the right to contract a marriage valid under Roman law with all its attendant rights and duties. More importantly, in day-to-day life it gave access to the Roman law, especially in regard to commerce

---

[6]Peter O'Brien, *The Epistle to the Philippians*, p. 3.

and property. He owed allegiance to Rome, and Rome would
protect him.[7]

Whether in Roman territory, or wherever the Roman citizen travelled
outside of Roman territory, Rome's responsibility was to protect its
citizens and their responsibility was loyalty to Rome.

Philippi was also a religious city of diverse nature with an influx of
people brought in from everywhere in the Mediterranean region and
Asia and other parts of Greece. Even though the letter does not say that
the church in Philippi existed side by side with many other religions,
we know, according to Acts, that there were other religions in the city
at the time, prominent of which was the Emperor Cult.[8] Bockmuehl
agrees that there were many cults apart from the official Roman cult.
However, only three were there in the first century:

1.   the unofficial folk religion, which was a cult for lower class men,
2.   the cult of Dionysus, also known as Baccus or Liber Pater, which
      promised eternal bliss to its worshippers and
3.   Racian Rider or Aulonite Hero, which was a knight on horseback.

Along with the official Roman cult, these were the cults that were
worshiped by the inhabitants of Philippi. Other cults like Diana and
the Egyptian cult came much later on.[9] Acts 16 also tell us that fortune
telling was also part of the life of the city.[10] Thus, Philippi, in terms of
religion, was no different from the other cities of the Roman Empire.

---

[7]Francis Lyall, *Slaves, Citizen, Sons: Legal Metaphors in the Epistles*, Zondervan, 1987.
p. 62, citing William W. Buckland, *The Textbook of Roman Law, Augustus to Justinian*,
pp. 96-98.
[8]Bockmuehl, p. 6.
[9]Ibid. Joseph A. Marchal, who mentions only Dionisus along with the cuts of Isis,
Diana,/Artimes and Silvanus, all female cults except Silvanus.
[10]See David E. Garland, p. 178.

According to Acts 16, backed up by archaeological excavations, Philippi had no synagogue when the gospel came into the city and even by the time of Polycarp in the second century. This confirms there were an insignificant number of Jews in the city, as you needed 10 male Jews to form a synagogue. Judaism, unlike Christianity, was a recognised religion, and its absence meant that Christianity would face greater opposition than might otherwise have been the case.

Acts 16 also gives some brief information about the coming of the gospel in the city of Philippi during Paul's second missionary journey. Acts agrees with historians that the city was a Roman colony (16: 12) in the Roman Province of Macedonia. This was Paul's first port of call in Europe after hearing the angelic call to come over into the Macedonian Province with the gospel.

Paul then must have been more than an evangelist or missionary, but a missionary-activist to preach in such a city, raise believers there and to later write as he did to the Philippian church. As a citizen, both of Rome and heaven, he did not see himself as a stranger and not even as a minority without a voice, as Christians often do today. Rather he took seriously his Roman citizenship using the rights and privileges a Roman citizen had to the fullest for the spread and establishment of the gospel in the Roman cities where he was able to plant the gospel. His being in the minority did not stop him from expressing his rights to speech, to hold a religion or belief and to share that belief or opinion without hindrance. Whether for Paul, or for believers today, this is what it means to be free and to be a citizen of an empire or a nation with all the rights and privileges thereof. If there is anything that Christians today have not taken advantage of, it is this right of a citizen of any country, at least for the sake of the gospel, if not for their own personal survival in the nation God has put them in.

According to the opening address of the Letter to the Philippians, the letter is written to the entire church in Philippi, to its bishops and deacons and all the members of the church or the saints. Why did he mention the members and bishops and deacons and not simply the presiding or leading bishop of the city or area, as we would do today? For Paul did not say, "To the church/saints in Philippi," but "to all the saints, bishops and deacons," just as he does in his other letters. By this, he meant to imprint on them the idea of working together in the gospel by specifically recognizing or mentioning all the categories of gospel partners. He gave a practical example of partnership when he referred to himself and Timothy, the authors of the letter in the opening address, which is, "From Paul and Timothy, "the slaves of Jesus Christ." By so doing, Paul gives us a gist of the subject of the letter in the opening address, as in his other letters. As we find in almost all ancient letters of the time, the address usually gives a highlight of what is in the body of the letter, in the same way as the thanksgiving portion had.

The thanksgiving portion of the letter leaves us in no doubt that Paul and the church in Philippi had a good rapport. The church in Philippi shared in Paul's missionary work, both in kind and cash, motivated by a deep sense of love for him. The tone of the letter shows the close friendship between Paul and the Philippian church, in contrast to what we find in his letters to the Corinthians or Galatians, for example. As such, the church was saddened to hear of his imprisonment. They demonstrated their sorrow and identification with his plight by sending practical support in the form of Epaphroditus to serve him while in prison, and financial support for Paul. Further Paul recalls how they supported him repeatedly while he was in Thessalonica (1: 3 - 12; 4: 10, 14 - 16, 18). Thus, Paul was constantly thanking God for his grace that was evident in their love for one another. He prayed that such love would increase more and more with knowledge and discernment (1: 9).

However, all was not well with the church. There was external opposition from unbelievers in town (1: 27 - 30). As a result, church members seemed to be frightened and confused how they should respond. Paul called for unity of purpose and steadfastness in the faith. There were also some internal problems in the church especially with the rise of false preachers and teachers more concerned about their credentials and the financial benefits that accrued to them from preaching the gospel than with faithfulness in the preaching of the gospel and love for those they ministered to (3: 2 - 6). In addition, some in the leadership of the church, like Euodia and Syntyche, disagreed about certain issues. Despite Paul not mentioning the area of disagreement, he pleads that both these female leaders should resolve the matter and that the church should help them to do so. It is not uncommon today to notice wrangling between some church leaders without the leadership or some members calling them to order. Very often, we talk about it in our corners but we do not venture to call the parties to order or reconcile them. Not so with Paul, not because he was a leader, but because of his theology of the church, his zeal for safeguarding the unity and salvation of believers in Christ.

The unity of the Philippian Letter

The integrity of the letter has not been questioned until recently. Those who do not agree that the letter is a unit, like Helmut Koester,[11] argues that the letter is not one single letter Paul wrote to the Philippian Church, but three (Letter A: 4: 10 - 20; Letter B: 3: 1b- to somewhere in chapter 4 and Letter C: 1: 1 - 3: 1a) and that they were composed

---

[11]Helmut Koester, Rd. K. Crim et al. "Philippians, Letter to the," in *Interpreter's Dictionary of the Bible: Supplementary Volume*, Nashville: Abingdon, (1976) p. 665.

into one by a later editor. However, he does not say, (1) who that editor is, (2) why the editor compiled the three letters into one and (3) why even after doing so we still have the problem we have, which the editorial work should have taken care of. Such scholars argue this way because they claim that there is no relationship between the soft Paul in Philippians 1 and 2, and the harsher tone seen in chapters 3: 2 - 4: 3. They say that there is no smooth transition formula or formulae from one subject matter to the other.

We need not spend time in arguing against those who do not see the unity of the letter. If there were originally three letters and an editor compiled them, then we would expect that they would have corrected the problems these scholars raise. Further, they are only causing more problems rather than solving whatever issues they believe question the unity of the letter. We will, therefore, simply go on here to show that the letter is a unit.

Note that Paul follows the normal writing letter writing style from the address, salutation and thanksgiving as in any ancient letter, with the addition of his Christian influence on the convention of letter writing of his day. Among his contemporaries, it was expected that such matters raised in the opening portion of the letter in the address would come up and be dealt with in the body of the letter. Thus, in the address, the issue here is the partnership or unity of the workers and members of the church in Christ, and the grace and peace of God within and among them all (1: 1 - 2). In the thanksgiving (1: 3 - 11), it is joy in prayer over their partnership or sharing in the gospel. He prays that this partnership continues until the return of Christ and that their love for one another may abound more and more with knowledge and insight and be pure and blameless until the day of Christ. As the Philippians read this introductory portion, they would have expected Paul to touch on the main issues raised in the letter's introduction.

Thus, broadly speaking, chapters. 1: 12 - 2: 30 deal with the issue of external opponents faced by both Paul and the Philippian church and the manner in which they are to approach these opponents. Chapters 3: 1 - 4: 9 discuss how to deal with internal opposition and strife. Then in 4: 10 - 20, Paul is seen as rejoicing and giving thanks to the Philippians for the gift they had sent. However, it is more than simply a thank you portion at the end of the letter, but a thank you for what they sent along with a lesson on Christian giving and receiving and contentment.[12] Based on this, its placement at the end is appropriate. In this way, the letter ends on a happy note and on a very important aspect of the Christian life, Christian giving, contentment and appreciation, made practical by the Philippians' giving and Paul's appreciation and contentment in the letter. In this way, the letter provides theoretical and practical advice on Christian giving and receiving, contentment and appreciation at the same time.

Looking closely at the letter in the light of ancient letters and Paul's other letters, the Letter to the Philippians appears well structured from opening to closing. As said earlier, the address and thanksgiving focus on the Philippian church's partnership in the gospel of Jesus Christ with Paul. This working together in the gospel entails sharing together in God's grace, grace that is both spiritual and material. It also entails love, which is expected to grow more and more with knowledge and discernment between right and wrong. Thus, Paul in this letter is concerned about the corporate or communal life of the church in Philippi. Certainly, they are not to live their lives as mere citizens of Philippi or Rome, because he says they are not to live in accordance with Roman law but in accordance with the gospel (1: 28), which is the law regulating the life of their heavenly state. It is in 3: 20 that he comes

---

[12]See below for a more detailed layout of the content of the letter.

out openly to say what and where their *politeuma* or citizenship is.[13] They are thus to conduct themselves in accordance with the lifestyle of their citizenship as stipulated by the gospel, in which they are partners with him.[14] How they are to do this is what Paul sets out in the body of the letter to achieve.

The transition from his address, salutation and thanksgiving to the body of the letter is shown by the transition formula, "I want you to know, brothers that …." (1: 12). In Phil. 1: 12 - 2: 30, Paul encourages the church in Philippi concerning their suffering at the hands of their external opponents. Here, he tells them that they are suffering for the sake of the gospel, that they are not alone in this and that it takes unity, humility, self-sacrifice and steadfastness to achieve the salvation envisaged in the midst of such opposition.

Paul begins his encouragement in the body of the letter by first citing his own experience in prison to show that he and they are suffering for the same reason (1: 30). He says that his imprisonment has revealed his innocence to the Palace guards as they realised that he was in prison for his faith and not for any crime. Probably this is what assures him of his release in due time. Secondly, he says that his imprisonment encouraged his fellow preachers to stand up for Christ and his gospel to the point of risking their own lives. They thought if Paul could do it, they too could do it as well. It did not matter to Paul that some were doing it for the wrong reason, so as to injure him. They took advantage of his imprisonment to raise their own level of popularity among the believers over and above his own. For

---

[13]Liddle & Scott, *Greek-English Lexicon: With Revised Supplement*, Oxford: Clarendon Press, 1996, sv.; Moulton, James Hope & Milligan, George, *The Vocabulary of the Greek Testament: Illustrated from the Papyri and Other Non-Literary Sources*, 1957, sv.
[14]Hermann Strathmann, Erlangen, "Polis, Polites Politeuomai. Politeia, Politeuma" in *Theological Dictionary of the New Testament*, (Ed.: Gerhard Friedrich), Vol VI, Grand Rapids:Eerdmans, pp. 516-535.

Paul, this action on their own part did not really matter, as long as Christ was being preached and people were being won for Christ and strengthened in their walk with Christ.

Paul's attitude here is a worthy example for today's pastors and preachers to emulate. Often it seems that what counts today is the name of the preacher and not the name of Christ Jesus. Moreover, because pastors are more concerned about their names, positions and material wellbeing, they spend endless time and energy castigating and side-lining one another, instead of struggling together with one mind and spirit to outwit the opponents of the church or of the cross. The result is that the gospel suffers and the enemies of the cross win the day. Unity in Christ is the answer to the problems of Christians today. We should conduct our lives according to the gospel, struggling together with one mind and one spirit, knowing that we are in the same suffering and in the hands of the same opponent. To do otherwise, is to allow ourselves to be destroyed by the enemies of the cross.

Paul wants to communicate this need for Christian unity to the Philippians. He starts with his own story. He wants to discourage any thoughts of giving up easily because of the enemy's intimidation. That is why he tells them he would not give up hope for his release from prison and he is seeing signs of this with the attitude of the Palace Guards and his fellow preachers. For this reason, he would rejoice continually and endeavour to exalt Christ in his body, whether he is released and stays alive or even if he is prosecuted and executed on account of the gospel. If it happens that he is prosecuted and executed, it is gain for him because he would rest from his labours and be with Christ. And if he is to be released and stay alive, it is equally Hallelujah, because it will enable him to bring fruitful service among them that will result in their progress and joy in the faith (1: 21 - 26).

After this, he picks up the subject of external opponents, using a very crucial statement, "Conduct your community life only according to the gospel of Christ," without allowing themselves to be intimidated by their opponents. This statement runs across the letter. His reason is that if they were community minded by consciously struggling together with one mind and spirit and not individually, their enemies would not be able to intimidate them. The result is that their own salvation would be evident and the destruction of their enemies would be apparent to them. Thus, just as he Paul has stood firm in Christ, so they too should stand firm because he and they are passing through the same suffering and from the hands of the same opponents.

He brings in the example of Jesus himself (2: 1ff) to encourage them to continue to strive to work together in the gospel of Jesus Christ. Partnership in the gospel entails humility and self-sacrifice for others, as Christ exhibited. There is exaltation at the end in considering the interest of others rather than in protecting one's own interest at all cost. It is in humility and not arrogance or a holier-than-thou attitude that one is exalted. Exaltation is in self-sacrifice for others and not in selfishness or "I first and others second." This is because life is for service and service is not working for self but for others in church and the larger society. When we exhibit this Christ-centred value, God and people around us, even those who may hate our lifestyle, exalt us. In contrast to typical attitudes in our African cultures or even in western cultures, the Christ-like way of life springs from a superior and not an inferior mind.

Another practical example used by Paul referring to working together in the gospel (vv. 22 - 30), is the life and ministry of Timothy and Epaphroditus. These godly men were servants of God known to both Paul and the Philippian Christians for their dedication to service in the work of the gospel (2: 19 - 30). By sending them to

Philippi, Paul is affirming the importance of their self-sacrifice in their partnership in the gospel with both Paul and the Philippians. Timothy and Epaphroditus would supplement what Paul is sending to the Philippians in writing both by their presence and by further explanations of the letter's contents.

What follows in 3: 1 - 4: 9, is about internal problems. The transition formula used here is, "The bottom line of it all, my brothers"(*loipon*) or "besides, my brothers," "moreover, my brothers," as rendered by Thayer.[15] This formula is used to both close the preceding subject matter, which is, suffering from the hands of external opponents and it is also used to transit to the new subject matter, that is, the internal opponents to be avoided (3: 2 - 4: 1) and the strife between two leaders in the church (4: 2 - 3). Since this is not the last subject matter in the letter, we cannot understand *to loipon* in the sense of "finally." or "lastly," but "the bottom line is, brothers" or "at the end of it all, brothers." In other words, whatever be the case, internal or external problems, "the bottom line of it all is, brothers, rejoice in the Lord always!" This will fit into what he has said and what he is going to say from now on.[16]

In this section, there are also examples put forward for the Philippians, but here they are negative examples to avoid. The negative examples are referred to as the dogs, the earthly bound or enemies of the cross. The other negative example is the disagreement between

---

[15] *Thayer"s Greek-English New Testament*, maintains that when the notion of time is dropped it can be understood as "besides, moreover, . . . forming a transition to other things to which the attention of the hearer is directed – Eph. 4: 10; Phil. 3: 1; 4: 8; 1 Thess. 4: 1; II Thess. 3: 1."

[16] Liddell & Scott, henceforth Bockmuel, p. 176, says, "the literal translation would include 'as far as the rest is concerned', 'and beyond that' and even 'and henceforth,'" but this rendering of the Greek *loipos*, is not very much different from "finally" and is not a fitting connector between the subject before and after.

Euodia and Syntyche. Paul, on the other hand, is perceived as the positive example to emulate.

Chapter three, verse one is not, therefore, introducing the closing matters, as some scholars presume. It is new in the sense that the opposition in this section is internal and not external, but it has to do with the same issue of being steadfast in the midst of opposition or problems. Paul is simply moving from talking about external opposition to Christian citizenship to internal opposition against the gospel. As such, the tone is supposed to change because if he is talking to the Philippian church to conduct themselves as Christian citizens according to the gospel and some are going in the opposite direction, then he cannot pretend that all is well or speak as if all is well. As he spoke harshly to the Galatians in such a situation, so will he do the same here. Paul is a frank and honest leader and preacher who calls a spade a spade, but still holding his peace and love for the church concerned. Frankness is still a quality of good leadership, especially today in a world being destroyed by insincerity.

In one verse (3: 2), Paul turns to the new set of opponents of the church he calls, "the dogs, evil doers and mutilators" who appear not to be three different groups of opponents within the church, but one, Jewish Christians who wanted Gentile believers to be circumcised so that they be accepted by God. In vv. 3-14, Paul asserts that he and the Philippians are the true circumcision; the people who worship by the Spirit of God; the people who glory in Christ Jesus and who put no confidence in the flesh (vv. 3). Then he goes on to narrate his Jewish background and zealous and perfect life as a Judaist based on the Torah (vv. 4-6). However, he gave up all of those achievements for the sake of Christ Jesus, that is, in order to know Jesus Christ, know the power derived from his resurrection, know what it means to share in his suffering and to become like him in his death (vv. 7-11).

Verses 12-14 explains what he said in vv. 7-11. He does not mean he has arrived, for he is still pressing on to take hold of what Christ took hold of him for, or what Christ called him for. He goes on in vv. 15-16 to say that he and those of them that are matured (using the same word used in v. 12) should take the view he has said. Nevertheless, that if in some issues some feel differently, God will make that known to them as well. However, all of them, including himself, must live up to what they have attained.

Having said all these about himself, about the matured and the need to hold on to what they have already attained, he moves on to v. 17 to call on the Philippians to observe from among them those who live as Paul and co-workers have set them an example. In vv. 18-19, he encourages them to take note of people who are good examples, for there are many who live as enemies of the cross, whose god is their stomach, who glory in their shame, who are earthly bound and so their end is destruction. In vv. 20-21, he returns to the state of the Philippians, himself and other Christians whom he says are citizens of heaven, whose lowly bodies will be transformed to be like Christ's glorious body.

Chapter four, verse one serves as a transition from what has been and what is to come. That is, it serves as a transition from believers who have become enemies of the cross by the way they live to believers who have not turned away but are not in agreement with each other.

Verses 2-3 belong to the section on the internal problems that are threatening the unity of the church. Paul appears to be transiting to a new subject by using one of his transition formulae, *Parakalo*, "I beseech/plead ...," it is still part of an opposition from within the church between two prominent leaders of the church, between Euodia and Syntyche. He calls on the two women to reconcile or agree. He calls a co-worker of his who is in Philippi to step into the matter and see that they are reconciled with another and so is the rest of the leadership. The call not to be anxious is to be seen within this context.

He goes on in vv. 4-7 to say that they should not be anxious about anything but rejoice in the Lord, allowing their gentleness to be known to all and not just within their community. Instead of being anxious, they are to take their petitions to God in prayer together with thanksgiving. The result is that they would experience the peace of God that surpasses all understanding. It would also guard their heart and minds in Christ Jesus.

Using again the transition formula, *oun liopon*, he moves on in vv. 8-9 to call on them to reflect on whatever is true, noble, right, pure, lovely, admirable, excellent or praiseworthy and to put into practice what they have learned, received and heard from him.

Chapter 4: 10 - 20 is the last issue in the body of the letter, introduced by the letter body transition formula, "I rejoice greatly that ..." This passage cannot be seen as a biographical epilogue or closing remark alongside the closing greetings, as Robert C. Swift asserts, for example.[17] This is because working together in the gospel is a central theme in the thanksgiving portion of the letter in 1: 3 - 8. Paul cannot simply bring the issue of sharing in material possessions, which is an aspect of partnership in the gospel as a closing remark when he has not dealt with it in the body of the letter. Moreover, the issues of giving thanks for the gift sent to him by the Philippians, of giving and receiving, of contentment, raised here are not merely passing comments but crucial theological statements that marked Paul's theology of giving and receiving. This same issue is treated in 1 Corinthians 16: 1 - 4 in a cautious but transparent way, and in a much more detailed way in 2 Corinthians 8 and 9, showing how important

---

[17]Robert C. Swift, "The Theme and structure of Philippians" in *Vital New Testament Issues: Examining New Testament Passages and Problems*, 1996. p. 177f.

sharing material possessions is for Paul, as it was in Greco-Roman era of his day. Because of its theological importance for Paul, it is in order that he treats it as a last subject matter for strategic reasons. Given the importance of working together in the gospel in the structure of the letter, and what sharing in material possessions in that gospel can do, it is right for Paul to leave this to the end of the body of the letter. Paul is aware of the implications of giving and receiving, whether in Greco-Roman culture generally, or for relationships between the church and individuals who preach the gospel with those members who are well to do. Paul will not treat their gifts lightly but gives them their rightful place in the body of the letter, and there is no better place to do this than at the end of the body of the letter. Paul is well aware that giving and receiving material possessions can raise the fortunes of the church and those who preach the gospel as well as ruin the fortunes of the church of God and its preachers. For this reason, he cannot treat it as an appendix or make it a part of his conclusion when he has not yet dealt with it in the body of his letter.

As in all of Paul's letters and other ancient letters, Paul closes the letter with the usual greeting and doxology in vv. 21-23, demonstrating the network of relationships existing between him and the Philippian Christians and between the Philippian Christians and those with Paul and the household of Caesar. This network of greetings affirms the partnership in the gospel that the address and the thanksgiving portion highlight at the beginning, which the body of the letter elaborates and expands.

The Letter to the Philippians is, therefore, one single letter, sent to the Philippian church through Epaphroditus. The first issue in the body of the letter is external opponents and Paul is exhorting them to live their lives in accordance with the gospel. Instead of being intimidated by the opponents, he urges them to be steadfast and united, focusing on their salvation, which is in sight. He approaches this by first using the example of himself sharing in the same suffering as they are, then by using Jesus Christ, the foremost example and then Timothy and Epaphroditus (1: 12 - 2: 30). He then exhorts them to beware of internal opponents and strife, centring on Jewish Christians who felt circumcision was necessary for salvation and on two of the leaders of the church, Euodia and Syntyche, who are not in good terms with each other. He does this by calling on them to be in peace and harmony in line with the way of the gospel. Then, he goes on to encourage them not to be anxious about anything but to be gentle knowing that the Lord is near. Because the Lord is near, they should rejoice and be gentle and prayerful, taking their requests and petitions to God whose peace is beyond understanding, and who will guard their minds in Christ Jesus. They should reflect on anything that is true, noble and worthy of praise. They should not simply speak about this, but they should also practice what they have learned, received and heard from him (3: 1 - 4: 9). Then comes the thanks and exhortation on the gift he has received from the Philippians that sums up the subject of partnership with them in the gospel and all that are related to partnership in the gospel in the body of the letter in 4: 10 - 20.

This is followed by his usual assortment of greetings to the Philippians and his benediction, all of which hinge on intimate relationship of the people of God in Philippians and elsewhere (4: 21 - 22).

Therefore, a look at the Letter to the Philippians in the light of the epistolary conventions, shows that nothing suggests the letter is not a single letter written to the church in Philippi by Paul while in prison.[18] We should study, therefore, the Letter to the Philippians as one single, friendly and intimate letter, written to a church Paul so much loved, and who loved him so much that they were willing to share and practically and financially support him in the preaching of the gospel. He thanks them for this and charges them to strive to do so right to the end, despite the nature of the forces that stand against them from within and without.

The significance of the Letter

The significance of the letter to the Philippians and to us today cannot be over-emphasized. Major points include:

1. The letter gives us a good example of a leader of the gospel who has a close relationship with church members. Paul commends the good work of the people he leads in ministry to others, acknowledging even the good work of contending preachers. He speaks of uniting members to one another, being contented and thankful for the material support of members and not being demanding or overbearing on members, as is the case with many pastors today. The Philippian church's zeal to support mission work and the worker should be emulated by members of every church today. The work of the gospel cannot continue without material support. This includes supporting the worker as an individual in the ministry so that he or she can focus on the work he or she has been called to do. Supporters should not take this material support as a reason to look down on full-time gospel workers. Neither should the support make full-time Christian

---

[18]This is recognized by D. F. Watson, *Rhetorical Analysis*, pp. 86-87 and Peter O'Brien, *The Epistle to the Philippians*, p.14, L. C. A. Alexander, "Hellenistic Letter-Forms and the structure of Philippian," *JSNT* 37 (1989), pp. 87-101.

workers feel inferior nor shy away from telling the truth so as to protect such support. Full-time Christian workers give through their work for the gospel, which is credited to them in their heavenly account, just as the financial donor is credited for his faithful giving. Similarly, full-time Christian workers should be transparent and faithful in transmitting the word of God to believers, in spite of the fact that their livelihood comes from those who hear them, since that is what will also be credited to their heavenly account. The fellowship and teaching in the church provides the spiritual and moral foundation on which believers can build their lives in the work place and the giving of their tithes and offerings shows the partnership there is. That is why it is a partnership in which there is the giving and receiving of the word, and the giving and receiving of material blessings by both parties. Thus, making no one either superior or inferior to the other because both are able to give and to receive and none of what we give originates from us but is graciously and freely given us by the God who so loves us in Christ Jesus.

2. Cordial and harmonious relationships between church members is something that a leader will never sacrifice for any reason, for our unity testifies to the larger society of the reconciling work of Christ. A cordial and harmonious relationship here on earth is a foretaste of what awaits us there in heaven. We cannot preach this reconciling work to others and then be at the neck of one another or tear the church or community of believers apart for one's own personal gain. We would be contradicting the gospel we preach and thus turning away our admirers from coming into the faith and partnership and expelling those who have just come in. Thus by contradicting what we preach and teach by our actions towards one another, we would have already destroyed what we preach

by our own hands and in our own very eyes and worse still at our own peril.

3.   The example of the humility and self-sacrifice of Jesus Christ has made us what we are. This remains the perfect example that no true leader or believer can brush aside and still be a Christian or leader of the gospel of Christ Jesus.

4.   The letter to the Philippians makes clear to us the importance of living out our Christian virtues. This is the mark of our distinctiveness as citizens of heaven (not what gives us salvation) and our Christian message to the people of the world. Prominent among the qualities that mark us out include: continual prayer life, partnership, sharing or working together in the gospel, purity, blamelessness, giving thanks, righteousness (1: 3 - 11), goodwill, fearlessness, courage, rejoice, faith, contending as one man, standing firm, being in one spirit and mind (1: 12 - 30), self- sacrifice, encouragement, love, comfort, fellowship, compassion, humility, selflessness, obedience, interest in people (2: 1 - 30), reconciliation, forgiveness, truth, noble, gentle, right, praiseworthy, admirable (4: 1 - 9), giving thanks, concern for one another, contentment, give and take, greetings (4: 1 - 22).

5.   The importance of Israel's example and the truth of Christ's work now so that the law and rules and regulations are not our ritual guide but Christ and his gospel. The church as a body, as well as individual Christians, ought to watch out for false teaching and preaching so that we do not slip away from Christ and his gospel. False teachings are on the rise in our churches today or threatening to take over our churches, if we have not yet been overtaken. For example, the attention of pastors and members of almost every church is turning to the attractive prosperity gospel that is so popular, while the gospel of the cross, no one wants to

hear or preach. Like Israel, we are slipping into the idolatry of all sorts and into observance of laws, rules and regulations as what marks us as Christians, instead of faith in God's saving work in the death of Jesus Christ and faithfully walking according to that gospel everyday of our lives.

Questions for further reflection and study

1. What in this letter makes you acknowledge that Paul is the author of Philippians?
2. Why is Philippians said to be a friendly letter?
3. Outline the purpose for the writing of Philippians and how important are they for Christians today?

OPENING ADDRESS AND GREETING, 1: 1 - 2

[1]Paul and Timothy, who are slaves of Jesus Christ, to all the saints in Christ Jesus who are in Philippi, together with the bishops and deacons.[2]Grace to you and peace from God our Father and our Lord Jesus Christ.

In Africa, letters, just as in letters elsewhere, serve as a bridge between people who are separated by distance. In community settings, where contact and knowing the welfare of each other is very important, people tend to use the following format of letter writing. The general pattern of a letter from an elderly person in the village to a young person from the same village working in the city may be as follows:

> From I Chief Yohanna Pam to you Teacher Andrew Walshak, with grace and hope that you and your family are well, just as I and my family are well. We are so happy to have received your letter and the news about the good health of your family and your place of work and the way God is using you at work and in the church you worship. We thank God for you and for the way you take God seriously in all you do. May God spare you for us always.
>
> After many greetings to you and thanks for what you sent to us and for how God is using you, I want to tell you that ...

Thus, just as seen above in Greco-Roman and Jewish Letters, one looks for five very important features in these letters. These are the writer of the letter; the recipient; their status in society; the nature of the relationship that exists between the writer and recipient of the letter and the prayer of the writer for the recipient. All these help to give force and importance to the letter for both parties. All of them help to signal what the subject of the letter is. This is true of the Letter to the Philippians, as one can see from the two opening verses of the letter.

We do not usually pay attention to these very important aspects of the letter in the New Testament because of the way we perceive letter writing today. Our letters today are much more business-like, even amongst family and friends with the exception, perhaps, of letters between a boyfriend and girlfriend. Hardly do those communicating begin by asking about each other's health or welfare, the family, the work, and of the welfare of relations etc. For the New Testament writers, however, these questions are critical for they succinctly tell us something about the content of the body of the letter by the way they are constructed or put together

As in Philippians and his other letters, Paul's point of departure with the conventions of letter writing of his day is the theological content and the varieties of approaches he employs in every letter he writes, based on the situations of his readers.[1]

Today, with the introduction of cell phones and the internet, most people are not as structured in their letter writing as this. The close feeling of intimacy and love that used to be expressed in friendly and family letters are no longer there. Ideally, however, letters should have a personal touch to them using the name of the recipient, and they should summarize what ties the sender to the recipient. These are

---

[1]See, Introduction samples.

features of this letter, even though there are issues to be dealt with that affect them all. Thus, the addresses are as follows:

a.   Paul and Timothy who are slaves of Jesus Christ, v. 1a;

b.   To all the saints, bishops and deacons in Philippi, v. 1b;

c.   Grace and peace from our God the Father and Lord Jesus Christ, v. 2.

Paul and Timothy who are slaves of Jesus Christ, v. 1a

In Philippians, the key idea is the partnership of the people of God in the gospel of Jesus Christ. This is evident from the start with the opening address describing Paul and Timothy as the co-addressors or co-authors of the letter who share the same status, "slaves of Jesus Christ." Paul makes a practice of mentioning co-authors in several of his letters (cf. 1 Cor. 1:2; 2 Cor.1:1; Col.1:1; Philemon 1; 1 & 2 Thess. 1:1). The way in which Paul addresses the letter shows Timothy is more than simply a secretary to whom the letter was dictated to but one who contributed to the content of the letter in no small way in spite of the use of the first person singular in several places.[2]

The slave status he attributes to himself and Timothy is something we gloss over because of its evil connotations or we romanticize the word, to use Lyall's word, without giving much thought to it. The New Testament writers used the word "slave" at a time when the institution of slavery was well grounded in Roman law and had a much deeper and richer meaning than for us Christians today.

---

[2] Lynn Cohick, 2013, p. 26, because of the use of the pronoun "I", says, "Perhaps, then, Timothy functions as Paul's secretary, so his own expressions intertwine with Paul's thoughts in this letter.

Some dislike using the word "slave" because they know that a slave was regarded as property and not a responsible human being whether by Roman law or in the early nineteenth century. A slave had no rights of his own, but owed total obedience to his master in everything. Roman masters had the power of life and death over their slaves. So what does Paul actually mean when he refers to himself and Timothy as slaves of Christ and not slaves of sin? We often use this term to refer to Christian believers and leaders without really understanding its true meaning. However, because they were using the term, the practical reality of which was something they daily experienced, it carried much more weight for them when they used it in connection with the relationship with Christ than it does for us today.

To refer to them as slaves of Jesus Christ, meant they both are bought by Christ's blood for service, loyal and dedicated service and not service as they wish. Paul is communicating two crucial ideas; (1) that he and Timothy were bought by Christ's blood, and (2) that they as preachers and leaders of the gospel are no longer free to do as they wish, but must listen to the Master, Christ Jesus. The word slave has to do with service for the Lord and has nothing to do with oneself or for oneself, one's own personal aggrandizement or enhancement. Since in status terms, they are both slaves, there is no superior or inferior among them. In Nigerian social understanding, Paul has so lowered himself, not simply to the level of Timothy, but far below where both of them are supposed to be perceived. Yet, as far as Paul is concerned, he was not lowering his position nor that of Timothy, but that he was saying that they really are slaves by their calling and life as leaders. As leaders of the people, they are supposed to be completely loyal and submissive to Jesus in the service of the people they lead. We must not be misled by the negative connotation of the word slave in our context and think that it has no positive connotation in Paul's usage.

Paul is saying that the word, *oulos* or slave has a place in the Christian life. The Christian is indebted to his or her fellow. We are meant to serve one another and our loyalty in service is not a personal choice but is mandatory, unquestionable. It is a part-and-parcel of the life of the Christian to serve others and not to demand to be served. Throughout his letters Paul champions this theology of servant-hood, not simply of leaders but also of believers in general.

Paul, therefore, did not feel he was humbling himself but he was being what he was supposed to be, because this is what Jesus really became, (see 2: 5 - 11). He came to earth, took the form of a human being, and died the death of a slave and of a criminal. Therefore, Paul did not feel he was doing anything abnormal. He felt the Philippians should do the same, serving one another, as their Lord demands of his followers, especially those who are leaders of his people (John 13: 12b - 15).

As slaves of Jesus Christ, Paul and Timothy are, therefore, partners in the service or ministry of Christ Jesus.[3] As slaves of Jesus Christ, they are not slaves of any human master but of the anointed Jesus, the Son of the living God. They are the slaves of the Saviour and Lord of their lives and of all who believe.[4]

Is this perception of leadership as slaves out of place in our context today, especially in Africa where status and hierarchy are seen as an inalienable culture or the whole system will collapse? The negative experience of slavery in Africa and the US and Europe means that no one sees anything positive about slavery. We understand the word in the sense of subjecting others to serve us, in a dehumanized way and against their wishes. Paul, however, uses the word in the sense

---

[3]My own translation.

[4]This title slave seems to be a title used by the early leaders of the church, for James used it to refer to himself as well in his letter (James. 1: 1).

of serving others for their own worth in a dignified way and as a worthwhile position. He is using the word metaphorically to mean self-giving or self-sacrifice for the building up of those in our care. Therefore, we should note Paul is using the word, not in connection with members of the church, but leaders, leaders stooping down to serve those whom they lead. The word is neither used here nor anywhere else in Paul to approve slavery, or hold others in servitude, bondage or captivity for personal pleasure or good as one's property. However, it is used of one who has been claimed by Christ to serve God's people unreservedly. Indeed, the church of God is a status-less church because both he who is first, second and third serve and all are servants or slaves, are accountable and loyal only to the Master.

To all the saints, bishops and deacons in Philippi, v. 1b

Paul again follows the epistolary convention. However, he goes beyond the convention of mentioning the recipients of a letter to giving a rich theological designation of his readers as, "all the saints," as well as "the overseers" and the "deacons." In this way, we see that the same idea of partnership in the address is also applied to the recipients of the letter.

The separation of "to all the saints" from the "overseers and deacons" has, however, puzzled scholars. Scholars like O'Brien note the difficulty in understanding why Paul should single out the overseers and deacon in the salutation.[5] We may thus understand, "to all the

---

[5]G. W. Hansen, p. 42; Peter T. O'Brien, p. 49f. O'Brien's position on this seems unclear. He quotes J. F. Collange, who appears to acknowledge the fact that he is mentioning the overseers and deacons specifically because he does not want to leave them in doubt that they and the members all have a hand in the problem and solution to what is happening in the church. (J. F. Collange, *The Epistle of Saint Paul to the Philippians*, Trans. A. W. Heathcote, London, (1979), p. 41.

sanctified members, together with overseers and deacons" in either of two ways.

a.   Firstly, Paul has emphasized the overseers and deacons since there is a problem between some members of the leadership he is going to address in the body of the letter.

b.   Secondly, by the use of "together with," Paul is saying that the overseers and deacons are part-and-parcel of the "saints."

The first option is preferable. This is confirmed by his use of "together with." We are, therefore, to understand his use of "all the saints" is intended to give emphasis, in the sense of "all the members" of the church, excluding the leadership.

The idea of partnership is made very clear by the church members' designation as *hoihagioi*, that is, "saints" or "the sanctified ones" in Christ. His use of "the sanctified ones" and "in Christ," shows that their sanctification is given, and not earned or merited by any act on their part. Since the idea of merit does not come into play in the use of the word, they all are qualified and equipped for the work of the gospel. Not only are they all sanctified by God in Christ Jesus, they are inseparably united to their fellow believers, not simply to those in Philippi, but to all believers found everywhere, as he says to them in his address in 1 Cor. 1: 2. They are a single and indivisible body of believers. This signifies the communal or corporate nature of their community, a Christian citizenship whose conduct is according to the gospel of Christ, not of Rome nor the colony of Philippi where they reside. They are not scattered or lonely individuals in a loosely related community, where everyone is on his own, climbing the ladder of social status unmindful or inconsiderate of who else is on the ladder, as if they simply belong to the earthly citizenship of Rome or of Philippi where this kind of conduct prevails. By so doing, Paul, right from the opening address, has distinguished the believing community in Philippi from the unbelieving Roman colony of Philippi.

Grace and peace, v. 2.

The greeting is a very important part of the opening of ancient letters. In general, the address of ancient letters, including letters found in the Bible, is followed by greetings to the recipients. Such greetings were not profuse. In ancient letters, including those found in the Bible, it is simply one word, "greetings," as in Acts 15: 23 and 23: 26, for example. Paul's own greetings are much more elaborate, as we have it here, full of his theology regarding the relationship of the people to whom he writes and the God they believe. As here, his greeting is usually: "Grace to you and peace from God our Father and our Lord Jesus Christ."

What do we understand by the words, "grace" and "peace"? Grace is favour, mercy, goodwill or kindness voluntarily shown to a person by someone. The Greek word used here is, χαρις, *charis*.

Some have seen the distinction simply as Paul combining the Greek and Jewish greetings in their languages. However, this is better understood as one of Paul's initiatives to go beyond typical Jewish and Greek greetings, to form a distinctive Christian type of greeting. It thus becomes Paul's own creation with an element of intimacy and community spirit, for it is, "grace and peace from God our Father and our Lord Jesus Christ," different from the conventional greeting of his time.

By the use of the word, "our" Paul shows that God the Father and the Lord Jesus Christ belong to both the recipients and the addressors and so he cannot be claimed to be the exclusive possession of one or a few among the believers in Philippi or elsewhere. This makes the language here inclusive. Both the addressors and the addressees are beneficiaries of what God the Father and Jesus Christ impart. Paul and Timothy are beneficiaries of the same grace and peace they wish for the Philippians, for one cannot give or wish to others what he or she does not have for himself.

Thus, Paul initiates a Christian letter greeting. He is not greeting in Greek and in Hebrew at the same time like, *charis humin kai shalom*, as we do sometimes do today when we want to impress a multi-ethnic audience that we know and recognize their distinctive languages.[6] Rather he is greeting entirely in the Greek language, which should make perfect sense to a Greek speaking audience like Philippi. However, just as Paul adopts a new format of address in his letter opening, distinct from the conventions, so does he introduce a distinct Christian approach in his greetings, using two important words conversant to his Greek speakers and natives, "grace and peace to you" *charis humin kai airene...*). For Paul, the grace and peace from God are the greatest things that have freely come to humankind. The peace of God that manifests in and among people, especially believers, is the result of what God's grace has done, without which human life and relationships would be in shambles. And because grace and peace are God's and come from him, they are freely given to all who believe in his gracious saving work in Christ Jesus.

---

[6]This is not to say that doing so is not right. The Holy Bible acknowledges our languages as identity markers and uses them to champion the cause of the gospel in all cultures, as we read in the story of Pentecost in Acts 2. When we use the ethnic or local language common to all in the area of our operation, we give the people a sense of belonging or recognition and the gospel message penetrates or carries the message much more forcefully than the use of a foreign language. The use of ethnic tongues as identity markers is a problem only when we use such to side-line or oppress those who do not belong. However, as legitimate as it is, we cannot assume Paul is doing the same thing here in his use of "grace and peace," as we do in our congregations as preachers and teachers today. To do that, we will be reading too much into the text.

Hence, the address and the greeting bring to our attention the themes that are going to be at the heart of Paul's discussion of the characteristics of partnership in the gospel in this letter. Fowl is therefore right when he says,

> Rather than explain how this standard greeting came to be, it is more important to recognize that it is a thoroughly Christian expression. It reminds us that this is a letter from Christians to Christians. Paul presumes this commonality and later in the epistle he will speak more about the nature and shape of the life he and the Philippians share in Christ.[7]

It may need to be said here that by saying, "the grace and peace of God our Father and our Lord Jesus Christ" be their experience, Paul was not saying that they were yet to have this grace and peace. Rather, he is saying that his prayer and wish for them every time is that they continue to experience this grace whose practical manifestation is peace or harmonious living with one another in Christ and in and for the gospel of Christ.

We should note that peace and grace are central in this letter, both of which are not merited but freely given by God. Paul insists that the church be steadfast, be of the same mind and spirit without being intimidated by their opponents. Such is a testimony to their sure salvation and a testimony to the sure destruction of their opponents. Moreover, this is not based on works on their part but because God is graciously working in them to make this a reality (1: 7, 28, 2: 13, 3: 9, 4: 13, 23). Further, the peace of God is also in the background to what he has to say in this letter. The peace of God does a lot in holding believers together whatever problems they face. Without the peace, which God filled Paul's mind with, he could have broken down spiritually,

------

[7]S. T. Fowl, *Philippians*, p. 15.

physically and psychologically. Given the many imprisonments Paul passed through along with all kinds of torture that accompanied Roman imprisonment, he could not have been able to cope without the peace of God upon his life. The peace of God gave him joy even in the midst of suffering. He was able to be confident that he would be out of it. He was also sure that his partners in the gospel were praying for him regarding his work and suffering. This peace made him not to worry about the envy of some fellow preachers of the gospel (1: 15 - 20). And it is through experiencing the grace and peace of God that enabled him to care less about himself and to care more about the gospel and the believers he was meant to build and strengthen (1: 17 - 18, 24 - 26, 2: 17, 4: 4 - 7). Moreover, because Paul believed that peace is an integral part of his life and teaching and God's gift to his church, he insisted on a cohesive and harmonious co-existence within and among the church members in the midst of a hostile environment (1: 27 - 2: 30). He was able to insist on watching out for those from within the church who would want to ruin this peaceful co-existence from God that he gives to his church, and to stand against personal gains (3: 2 - 4, 18 - 19, 4: 2 - 3).

It is therefore evident that, the letter opening of Philippians has already put forward to the recipients what the subject(s) of the discussion in the body of the letter is going to be. As Hansen puts it,

> In his opening greetings, Paul begins to express the main points of his letter. His inclusion of Timothy in a partnership of servants of Christ Jesus, his inclusive address to all in Christ Jesus, and his rewording of the **Shema** to include the Lord Jesus Christ with God the Father as the common source of grace and peace introduce the themes of the gospel of Christ and the community in Christ."[8]

---

[8]G. W. Hansen, *The Letter to the Philippians*, p. 43.

We thus can understand why Paul ends the address with his usual Christian greeting of "Grace to you and peace from God our Father and our Lord Jesus Christ." By wishing them this unmerited grace and peace of God, Paul is saying, that as beneficiaries of God's unmerited favour and reconciliatory work in Christ, they are to relate to one another, through the same grace and peace of God, without which true partnership in the gospel is impossible. Moreover, because this is meant to be an introduction to what is in the body of the letter, this desire for gracious and peaceful partnership in the gospel, which should be seen in their daily living, runs throughout the issues raised in the body of the letter.

Questions for further reflection and study

1.   Why is greeting so important for Paul at the beginning of his letters and how important is this for the Christian today?
2.   What is so important about the address in 1:1?
3.   What do we learn from the manner in which the recipients of this letter are addressed in 1:1b?
4.   Discuss the salutation in 1:2.

UNIT 3

THANKSGIVING AND PRAYER, 1: 3 - 11

Very rarely do people thank God for the good found in others. Yet such thanksgiving is a good thing to do and everybody loves to hear Christian leaders thanking God for what church members do in serving God. However, due to other distractions, Christian leaders seldom thank God for their members' service to God. Yet, this is a very important part of human life. Not only does it boost the morale of the people whose service is being appreciated; it also encourages those doing the thanking. Above all, giving thanks in prayer to God for what other Christians are able to do, unites the one giving thanks and the parties concerned in an intimate way.

As previously mentioned, thanksgiving in a letter is as characteristic of Paul as it was in Greco-Roman letters of his day. The thanksgiving portion of a letter in Paul's time was a very important feature because it expresses the joy and appreciation of the writer concerning the good in the recipient.[1] With the exception of Galatians, the thanksgiving part

---

[1]See P. Yamsat, 'Thanksgiving' in *The Ekklesia as Partnership: Paul and Threats to Koinonia in I Corinthians*, Ph.D. Dissertation, University of Sheffield, Sheffield, England, 1992, pp. 12f, citing, P. Schubert (1939), p. 26f; Peter O'Brien, *Introductory Thanksgiving in the Letters of Paul, Supplement to NovumTestamentum 49*, Leiden

of Paul's letters, in conjunction with the opening address, highlights the content of the letter, thus making it a very significant part of the letter. The fact that the Galatian letter is introduced with a rebuke portion instead of a thanksgiving portion, suggests that Paul didn't feel all of his letters had to have a thanksgiving section. Whether a thanksgiving or rebuke section introduced the letter depended on the nature and purpose of the letter. Since Galatians is not our focus here, it is enough to say that an introductory rebuke portion in Paul's letter shows his displeasure over the change of mind of the recipients of his letter, whereas in an introductory thanksgiving portion, he shows his joy and appreciation over the good evidenced in the readers of his letter. A letter of rebuke is also not uncommon in Greco-Roman letters, as scholars have observed.[2]

Thanksgiving was a common feature in Greco-Roman letters. The addressor would normally give thanks to the gods concerning the addressee or recipient of a letter, stating his reasons for the thanksgiving being offered. We have letters with thanksgiving like that sent by Isias to her husband, Hephaistion in about 168 BC.[3] Prayer to

---

(1977), pp. 8, 10; C. J. Roetze, *The Letters of Paul: Conversation in Context*, London (1983), pp.33ff; D. E. Aune, *The New Testament in its Literary Environment*, 1987. 186.

[2]Gary M. Burge, Lynn Cohick and Gene L. Green, *The New Testament in Antiquity*, Zondervan (2009), p. 271, notes that the rebuke letter "was sent to someone who failed to follow instructions or foolishly changed his mind" and that there was usually a close relationship between the sender of the letter and its recipient, citing, a letter between a father and his son, P. Oxy. I 123.5-9, which reads: "I am very astonished [*thaumazo*], my son, that till today I have not received any letter from you, telling me about your welfare"; David E. Aune, 1987. p. 207.

[3]P Lond 42 (=UPZ. 59); Sel Pap 112, p. 305 (=BGU 432), second century (A.D.) Letter Written by Apion to his father Epimachos, cited by J. L. White, *Light from Ancient Letters*, 1986. p. 145; O'Brien, p. 54, who cites Schubert, pp. 158-179.

the gods for the recipient's welfare usually followed the thanksgiving portion of the letter.[4]

Just as in the Greco-Roman letters where the grounds for the thanksgiving are given, so we find the grounds for thanksgiving here in Paul's letter to the Philippians. However, even though Paul is very conventional regarding his thanksgiving in this letter he is not conventional in the content or grounds for his thanksgiving.. The content of his thanksgiving is unlike what we find in Greco-Roman thanksgiving. Paul's own is usually theologically worded and dependent on the kind of good obtainable in each church. Another thing worth mentioning is that the thanksgiving in Paul, as we have seen in the address, does give a highlight of the content of the body of the letter, as in ancient letters or speech.[5] Paul also departs from the conventions of thanksgiving in that he does not subscribe to rhetorical gimmicks in his own thanksgiving. He is rather sincere about whatever good things he says about his recipients. Hence, the content of his thanksgivings vary from letter to letter, albeit with some overlapping themes. Thus, the thanksgiving is a part of the letter's introduction along with the address and prayer. As Hauck puts it, "The Prescript in 1: 1 - 2, with its unique mention in the authentic Pauline corpus of "bishops and deacons" in the adscription and the thanksgiving with a concluding intercession in 1: 3 - 11 combine to form the letter opening."[6]

Here in Philippians 1: 3 - 8, Paul says that he continually thanks God in all his prayers for their partnership with him in the gospel of Jesus Christ, from the beginning when the gospel came to them up to the time of writing this letter (vv. 3 - 5). This partnership, he is sure, God

---

[4]See J. L. White, 1986.
[5]Markus Bockmuehl, p. 57; O'Brien pp. 58-61; Witherington p. 38
[6]Hans-Joseph Klauck, *Ancient Letters and the New Testament*, p. 31

will bring to completion in the day of Christ's return. (v. 6). Verses 7-8 express Paul's intimate feelings about the Philippians. He holds them with deep affection, the affection of Christ. In addition, in vv. 9 - 11, he offers prayer to God that the Philippians' love for one another and for him should grow more and more in knowledge and discernment and not just by emotion. For this reason, the purpose of his prayer is that they become pure and blameless, filled with the fruit of righteousness through Christ in the day of his return, all of which are not to their own glory, but to the glory and praise of God the Father.

Thus, the issue of partnership with one another and with Paul in the gospel becomes much clearer in the thanksgiving than in the address and will become much more evident in the body of the letter. Paul observes that whether he was in prison or defending or confirming the gospel anywhere, the church in Philippi would always work together with him, not only in the preaching of the gospel, but also in their finances as the Greek word, *koinonia,* conveys both the relational and monetary implications of partnership between two parties (cf. 4: 10 - 20).

The Thanksgiving, 1: 3 - 8

I give thanks to my God concerning you every time I remember you. [4]Always in all my prayers for all of you, I pray with joy, [5]because of your partnership in the gospel from the first day until now. [6]Confident of the fact that he who began this good work in you will bring it to completion until the appointed time of Jesus Christ.

[7]It is right of me to think this [way] about all of you, because I have you in my heart. Also in my imprisonment and in the defence and confirmation of the gospel, all of you were my fellow-partners in the grace [of God]. [8]For God is my witness,

> how I long for all of you with the innermost affection of Christ Jesus.[7]

The thanksgiving in this letter is centred on the partnership in the gospel with Paul by the Philippian church. This sense of partnership excites him and it is this partnership that shapes the entire letter. It is a gospel partnership both with one another and with Paul, which should encourage them to struggle together steadfastly, with one mind and spirit despite attempts by their opponents to intimidate them. For Paul, this is critical to keeping their salvation in sight. Moreover, this cannot be any less critical for leaders and members of our churches given the worldwide attacks against Christianity. The survival of the church, and the salvation of Christians, is dependent on churches working together with one another to overcome their opponents. We should not merely pay lip service to our unity, thinking this terrorism is bound to happen being the end of the age, or believing that despite a lack of action that the Lord will not allow them to destroy the church. The church has already been destroyed in many parts of Europe, North Africa and the Middle East, so there is no reason why it will not be destroyed elsewhere in the twenty first century, if churches do not holistically partner with one another in all that pertains to the gospel.

Some Christians and church leaders fail to give thanks for what is good in others for fear they will brag and fall. However, giving thanks to God or even the people concerned for the good in them boosts their morale, encourages them to do more, and assures them that they are on the right track. Giving thanks for the good in others does not mean that they have arrived spiritually or they are perfect but that they are doing well in their walk with God and that the thanks is meant to ginger them to do more and not to go to sleep.

---

[7]My translation.

Paul, therefore, makes it very clear to the Philippians in vv. 3-5 that he gives thanks to God every time he prays for them. As O'Brien noted, it is not that he continuously gives thanks to God but that every time he prays to God, he gives thanks on their behalf.[8] Not only that, whenever he prays for them, he does so with joy. Verse 4 makes it clear that he is not selective in the prayer of thanksgiving but he gives thanks for **all** of them whenever he prays. Paul's emphasis on the communal life of believers has already been acknowledged in his address, "Paul and Timothy, slaves of Christ" "to all the saints with bishops and deacons." This is re-affirmed here in the thanksgiving and its importance will be shown in the issues raised in the body of the letter. Joseph A. Marshall is therefore right when he says that Paul's use of the term *ouloi* (i.e. slaves) in 1: 1b to describe Timothy and himself has possible association with the hymn in 2: 1 - 11.[9] Verse 5 gives the reasons or grounds for why he always gives thanks to God every time he remembers them, and why he is always full of joy in his prayers for them. There are three grounds for his giving thanks to God on their behalf, two in v. 5 and one in v. 6. He gives thanks

1.   Because of their concern and remembrance of him;

2.   Because, whenever they had the opportunity, of their partnership with him in the gospel from when he arrived in Philippi up to the time of writing, and

3.   Because he is confident that God will bring to completion the good work he has started in them when Christ returns. This will include what they have done, as well as their concern and partnership, all of which are made possible through God's power in Christ.

---

[8]See O'Brien, Witherington and Martin on the opposite view.
[9]Joseph A. Marchall, pp. 119f.

Some see his use of "until now," to mean that he wonders if they will continue in the future, considering the issues to be raised that were likely to obstruct a continuous partnership, if they did not take care.[10] However, v. 6 appears to counter this impression as it shows Paul is sure that God will bring to completion the good work he has started in them.

What is the good work referred to here, which Paul is confident that God will complete on the day of Christ? Paul has already stated it in v. 5, that this good work is their partnership in the gospel from the time they received it until the time of his writing. Some scholars want to limit this to being merely the spiritual gospel they had received, which they continued to share in with Paul and each other.[11] Others limit it to the financial support they continued to give to Paul from the beginning of their conversion up to when the letter was written. However, Paul does not specify either option. If it only has to do with the Philippians' financial partnership with Paul, it is pointless to dichotomize the spiritual and financial partnership in the gospel when Paul is silent about it. This is much more so when it is located in the thanksgiving portion of the letter, which outlines all the themes to be raised in the body of the letter. Paul will not downplay any aspect of this partnership in the gospel in his thanksgiving. (We will discuss this further in 4: 10 - 20). Paul, therefore, is confident that when Christ returns God will bring to completion this partnership, which they began with him, and are still participating in, from when they first received the gospel. His confidence is in God to bring it to completion,

---

[10]Ibid. 120f.

[11]See, G Fee, pp. 86f, because Fee says that this is so because Paul does not say "good work through you" but that the "accent "is on what God is doing in (or among) them, not what he is doing through them. But this makes little difference as long as God remains the main actor in both and gets the credit for both. Fowl (p. 26), says it is God's act of "bringing the Philippians into the economy of salvation").

not the Philippians' abilities. This feeling of confidence in God is not limited to a few among them but extends to all of them. He is confident that God will perfect this partnership in the gospel by God's own power and grace at the return of Christ. As Bockmuehl puts it, it is rooted in the "character of God who unfailingly accomplishes what he sets out to do. Fee rightly stresses that 'this confidence has very little to do with them and everything to do with God, who both 'began' a good work in them and will 'bring it to completion' at the day of Christ."[12] In his imprisonment, defence and confirmation of the gospel, all of them had been partners with him. Thus, while God is working in them, they too are working hand in hand with Paul to bring it to the perfect stage God wants it to be at the return of Christ. Hence 2: 13, where he asks them to work out their own salvation with fear and trembling.

Verses 7-8 shows Paul's own feeling about them regarding their concern for him, although he has already expressed this in his prayers for them. In vv. 7 and 8, Paul realizes that this very intimate language of his concerning his relationship with the Philippians may be thought to be too good to be true. It may be thought to be his own kind of *captatiobenevolentiae* - a concept that was very common in ancient speech, and is often used at the opening (*exorium*), to woo the audience to the speaker's side thus enabling the writer to win the good will of his listeners or readers. Paul, therefore, thought, "Who would know that I am sincere about these feelings of closeness that I have been expressing about them?"

However, we need to ask, is Paul saying the same thing by his use of "partnership in the gospel" in v. 5 and "my partners in the grace" in v. 7?[13] It would appear that in v. 7 Paul is giving a further explanation

---

[12]Bockmuehl p. 61; G. Fee. p. 86.

[13]Not "in my grace," for the article goes with grace, as Marshall, Silva and others propose. See, O'Brien; Fee, p. 91 n. 88; See M. Bockmuehl who rightly says that the

of what he said in v. 5, that to be partners in the gospel is far more than simply sharing in the good news of salvation. He is as well saying it also has to do with sharing in God's unmerited favour or blessings, which are both spiritual and material. They have shared with Paul in the preaching of the gospel he has been called to and have also shared with him their own material possessions. This fits in with the Greek use of *koinonia*. When *koinonia* and its cognates are used, they usually convey both the relational and monetary implications of such a relationship between the parties. By identifying with Paul in both good and bad times, in the spiritual and the material grace (*charis*) of God, Paul became deeply attached to this church "with the affection of Christ." This also fits in with what he will say in 4: 10 - 20.[14] Although M. Bockmuehl says that "partnership (*koinonia*) in the gospel" and "my partners in God's grace" "is certainly spiritual in nature," he however, goes on to say,

> But this spirituality has found its concrete expression both in
> the Philippians' participation in the task of proclamation" (v. 7)
> and in their repeated financial contribution to Paul's mission
> (4: 15); indeed the same idea of evangelical sharing can have

---

syntax is indeed ambivalent, and that an anterior placement of the possessive pronoun mou is grammatically possible, but goes on to say, "On balance, however, "my partners" is somewhat more likely both on syntactical grounds and in the oral context of a public reading: in the case of ambiguity, the more common Greek usage would prevail in associating "of me" with the preceding noun (as also in v. 8 'God is my witness)." A native Greek speaker like John Chrysostom shows no doubt that this is the right reading. p. 63.

[14]See G. Fee (p. 91) who says that in the light of 1: 29, "where the verb of this noun occurs in conjunction with their mutual suffering in Christ, Paul very likely is referring to the 'grace' of being 'partners together in the defence and vindication of the gospel even in the midst of present chains," which Fee admittedly says will include the Philippians financial sharing with him at his time of need in prison as well as their own suffering with Christ referred to in 1: 30, p. 92.

> clearly financial implication elsewhere (Rom. 15: 26; 2 Cor. 9: 13).[15]

Fowl also acknowledges the financial aspect of Paul's use of *koinonia* and rightly observes that Paul incorporates all aspects of his relations with the Philippians under the rubric of *koinonia*."[16] While we may emphasize the spiritual aspects of working together in the gospel here, we cannot belittle the financial sharing aspect of the partnership, which is found in the thanksgiving, especially when Paul uses *koinonia* in this thanksgiving portion of his letter. As mentioned before, the thanksgiving is supposed to highlight the themes raised in the body of the letter.[17] We should note that apart from the fact that *koinonia* is used both in relational and financial transactions or matters; Paul does not dichotomize the Christian life into spiritual and physical categories, as many Christians are prone to do today. (This problem has unfortunately led to the lack of Christian influence in the wider society today). Whenever the word *koinonia* is used in the thanksgiving, we expect that some financial transaction is involved and that the issue of financial sharing, and other aspects of sharing, are going to appear. In v. 7, Paul is, therefore, saying that it is right, just, or lawful (*dikaios*) for him to think and be moved (*phronein*) the way he has, because whether he was in prison or preaching the gospel, they partner with him.

In v. 8, Paul realizes that the intimate language he employs concerning his relationship with the Philippians may be perceived as being too good to be true. To explain to them further the sincerity of his thanksgiving and intimate feeling about them, he says in v. 8 that only God is his witness concerning the fact that he has all of them in

---

[15]M. Bockmuehl, p. 60.

[16]S. E. Fowl, p. 22f.

[17]Fowl, p. 24; See also G. Fee, pp. 83-5 who seems to be shifting from only sharing in spiritual gospel to sharing in everything including financial, like Fowl.

his heart and longs for all of them with the innermost affection that originates from Christ. In the gospel of Christ, he and all of them have been partners, are partners, and will be partners until the return of Christ Jesus. Only God, who knows the hearts of people, can testify to the fact that he truly has all of them in his heart and not just some "favourite individuals or groups."[18] He goes further in this verse to use a far more intimate and affectionate expression to show his feelings for them. He says that he longs for all of them "with the innermost affection *(splangchna)* of Christ Jesus." Paul has gone to his limit by turning to God and Christ Jesus to convince them about the kind of love he has for them by saying that he loves them with the kind of deep or bowel love that Christ Jesus has for them. It is a love that originates and comes only from Christ. This love is made plain in his discussion of the Philippians' need to emulate the humility and self-sacrifice of Jesus in 2: 1 - 11 and his thanksgiving for their gift to him in 4: 10 - 20.[19] As a result, he goes on in vv. 9-11 to show them the prayers he offers continually to God on their behalf.

That love would increase, 1: 9 - 11

> [9]And this I pray, that your love may still increase more and more with knowledge and all discernment [10]that you may discern what is best, that you may be pure and blameless in the day of Christ, [11]having brought to completion the fruit of righteousness through Jesus Christ to the glory and praise of God.

---

[18]M. Bockmuehl, p. 65.

[19]See M. Bockmuehl (p.65) who understands "the source and occasion of Paul's affection are not in himself nor in the Philippians" goes on to say, "John Chrysostom suspects that the phrase dispels any thought that Paul loves the Philippians only for their partnership with him. Instead, the source is the passionate and compassionate love of Christ."

In v. 9-11, Paul now returns to the prayer that he started in v. 6. Since all that Paul has said about the Philippians, and all that the Philippians have shared with Paul has been generated by their love for one another, and since this mutual love comes from God, Paul prays to God that this love grows or increases with knowledge and discernment. If their partnership in the gospel must continue to the end, it must not remain stagnant, but it must increase. Moreover, it must not only increase, but increase in knowledge and discernment. A love that does not grow, that is dwarfed or stagnant, stems from emotions or sentiments, but a love that grows in knowledge and discernment is solid and firm, unshaken by difficult circumstances. Partnership and love rooted in knowledge is able to discern, distinguish and understand things that are, and does not fade away, even in difficult times, (eg vv. 12-26). This partnership, and what they are going through, enables him to ask them to be steadfast in the midst of suffering in 1: 27 - 30, to be self-sacrificing in 2: 1 - 4, to look to Jesus Christ, who withstood humiliation and was exalted 2: 5 - 11. This mutual love makes him call on them to withstand the false teachers and prophets from within the church (3: 2, 18f) and to press on despite their circumstances, until they reach perfection at the return of Christ (3: 7 - 14).

Therefore, in v. 9 Paul tells the Philippians how he prays to God on their behalf, not for what they do not already have, but for the deepening of what they are already doing. He says he is praying, "that your love may still increase more and more with knowledge and all discernment." Love that is not based on facts, awareness, or good judgment, but on sentiments or emotions, hardly grows or increases. It may rather disappear with time when the thing that stirs it dies or diminishes. However, when our love for others is guided by knowledge and discernment, we are bound to recognize and approve whatever is excellent and disapprove what is not, any time and any day under any condition. O'Brien says,

> Paul prays that the love of the Philippians might overflow within the domain of 'knowledge and all insight' ... His earnest desire was that there be no limit to the growth or increase of the Philippians' love and in order to stress the idea of continuous growth he used the progressive present tense, περισσευη.[20]

This increase of their love in knowledge is not solely intellectual or head knowledge of God, but one that shows itself in good practical relationships. That is why it is a love that grows in knowledge and discernment, or insight, or "tact," or "the feeling for the actual situation at the time."[21] Paul said to the Corinthians that knowledge puffs up but love builds. Thus, the love referred to is the love that knows what is the right thing to do, discerns how best to go about it, and then puts it into practice with one another, with God and in every sphere of their lives.

Paul's prayer then was not that some fresh elements such as knowledge and insight might be introduced in their love as though these were two separate ingredients that were lacking or different. Rather, the content of the petition was that the love of God within the readers might increase beyond all measure, and that as it increased it might penetrate more deeply into personal relations with God through Christ as well as into all aspects of situations involving practical conduct.[22]

Verses 10 and 11 goes on to show that the purpose of all this is to bring the Philippian believers to completion or perfection at the return of Christ, filled with the fruit of righteousness that comes

---

[20]O'Brien, p. 75.

[21]As (aesthesis) translated, by R. P. Martin and E. Kasemann, respectively, cited also by O'Brien.

[22]O'Brien, p. 77.

through Christ Jesus to the glory and praise of God the Father. Love based on knowledge and discernment enables one to distinguish and recognize what is best, as Christ would want, and not simply what is good and bad. And the purpose for knowing what is best is not merely for the purposes of head knowledge or the intellectual ability to recognize what is best but so that the Philippians would be able to live pure (*eilikrines*) and blameless (*aproskopos*) lives and bear the fruits of righteousness, ready for the return of Christ. Thus, they will live so that others will not stumble. For Paul, this blamelessness is the most crucial thing. The purity and blamelessness of the Christian as he or she stands before God at the return of Christ is what counts most for Paul, and not so much what we do here and how we do it. It is crucial only as far as it makes us to be pure and blameless on that day. However, v. 11 goes on to say that this does not mean that what we do here does not count, for he has already said that it is our ability to distinguish between the best and choose to do the best that makes us blameless. His prayer is that as they increase in the love which enables them to know and discern what is best, and thereby become blameless, they will stand at the return of Christ filled with fruits of righteousness, fruits which originate from a righteous life that is made possible by the gracious work of God in Christ Jesus. That is why, as his doxology states at the end of v. 11, Paul gives glory and praise to God. For it is only by the power of God that either the Philippians, or believers today, are enabled to remain steadfast in our partnership in the gospel with one another.[23]

Thus, partnership is not a one-sided thing for Paul but a two-way thing, involving giving and receiving. Paul, on his part, always gives thanks to God for their partnership in the gospel, a partnership that is spiritual and material. He also prays to God that such partnership

---

[23]Bockmuehl, p. 70f.

and love for one another and for him be continually increased in all of them and in all aspects of life. This is his way of reciprocating their good gesture and God's gesture to towards us. He does this in a more elaborate way in the last subject matter of the letter, in 4: 10 - 20, in his appreciation for their practical expression of partnership through sending him financial gift.

Paul, thus, has been able to summarise in the address, greeting and thanksgiving what he is going to put forward to the Philippians in the body of his letter. Paul and his Gospel partner Timothy are but slaves with no rights of their own, except what Christ lays in their hearts to do. The Philippians, on the other hand, are all saints in Christ, whether they are members, bishops, or deacons in the church in Philippi. Their saintliness, their attainment to this status is in Christ and not in themselves or their hard work, as the citizens of the empire might claim. Their own status is the result of God's own gracious doing or work in Christ. He has enabled their partnership in the gospel with Paul. Moreover, it is he who will bring this good work that he has started in them to completion or perfection at Christ's return, in spite of their suffering from the hands of governing authorities. The gospel will triumph despite internal problems caused by materialism, or cravings for popularity and falsehood that seek to divert believing communities from Christ and the joy of being citizens of heaven.

Questions for further reflection and study

1.   Is giving thanks for what we receive from others necessary today and why?
2.   Discuss the merits and demerits of giving and receiving in the New Testament and today.
3.   Why did Paul receive from the Philippians so many times but could not from the Corinthians and what do we learn from this for our time?
4.   What is your theology of giving and receiving and how is that different from Paul's?

THE CHRISTIAN CONDUCT IN THE FACE OF PERSECUTION, 1: 12 - 2: 30

The story of the Tower of Babel shows us that unity is the most important factor in a society wanting to grow and develop. The people of Babel agreed among themselves to make bricks and build a city with a tower reaching the sky in order to make a name for themselves, and that they live in one place and not be scattered all over the earth. They started in earnest and God observed that nothing would hinder them from achieving their dream of building a magnificent city and a tower reaching heaven. God observed that not only would they be able to do this but they could also achieve anything they desired, since they were all united in vision and language. The only way to stop them achieving their vision was for God to divide them by creating different languages among them so that they may not understand one another. This forced them to scatter all over the place instead of being in one place to continue their project (Genesis. 11: 1 - 9). Unity, therefore, holds a community together both in good times and in hard times. It is such a great thing that it can enable people to achieve the impossible.

However, mankind did not create or invent unity. It is God's creation in Jesus Christ our Lord, through whom everything was created and without whom nothing could have been created (John. 1: 3). He is the one who prays the Father that all believers in him be united, as he and the Father are one (John. 17: 20-23). Yet unity also requires the involvement of people. Without love, self-sacrifice and steadfastness on the part of the people of the gospel, especially in a hostile world, there can be no unity.

In this section, Paul stresses the importance of an unwavering unity in the church of God in Philippi. He calls on them to conduct their community life in a way that is worthy of the gospel of Jesus Christ. Side by side, and without being frightened by opposition, they are to strive together as a community of believers in the work of the gospel and in their struggle against the gospel's opponents. For without unity, they cannot overcome their opponents and cannot gain the promised salvation. This is anchored in the word of God in Ecclesiastes 4: 9 - 12, thus:

> [9]Two are better than one,
> because they have a good return for their work:
> [10]If one falls down,
> his friend can help him up.
> But pity the man who falls
> and has no one to help him up!
> [11]Also, if two lie down together, they will keep warm.
> But how can one keep warm alone?
> [12]Though one may be overpowered,
> two can defend themselves.
> A cord of three strands is not quickly broken (NIV).[1]

However, this unity, this striving together with one mind and spirit is not achievable without mutual love, humility and self-sacrifice within

---

[1]The Mupun of Nigeria would say, *Vul a long, mishik a muut*, that is, "Two is wealth but to be alone is death."

the community of faith. It cannot be achieved by each championing his or her own self-interests but by working and walking together (2: 1 - 4). Jesus is the Christian's supreme example of this (2: 5 - 11).

Paul's experience, with which he opened the body of the letter in 1: 12 - 18, is not an isolated topic but belongs to the first subject of the letter, i.e. the suffering of the Philippian church, at the hands of their external opponents, of which Paul himself is a victim (1: 12 - 2: 30).[2] Hence, he used his story and prison experience (1: 12 - 18) to introduce the Philippian church's suffering, to show that they should follow his example of facing suffering from the hands of the same opponent (1: 30). He starts by showing them that his imprisonment has turned out to be for the progress of the gospel, because the Palace Guards on duty in the prison had come to realize that his imprisonment is for his faith and not for a crime. Further, his suffering has raised up zealous preachers who preach fearlessly. Even though some do it for the wrong reason, particularly to injure him, that did not matter as long as Christ was preached. Even though the choice between either freedom to continue the spread of the gospel or execution, and thus being with Christ, was a difficult one, he finally chose to be released for their progress in the faith, although personally he would have preferred to be with the Lord (1: 12 - 26).

He then turns to exhort them over their own suffering at the hands of external opponents, calling on them to conduct their communal life in accordance with the gospel, be steadfast, united and fight together with one mind and spirit with their salvation in sight, without being intimidated by their opponents. In this struggle, self-interest is not the thing but humility and self-sacrifice; taking care of each other's

---

[2]Hans-Joseph Klauck, *Ancient Letters and the New Testament: A Guide to Context and Exegesis*, Waco, Texas, 2006, p. 319, who says Paul's self-recommendation in 1: 12 - 26 provides the opening body as against Swift who sees it more as an introduction.

interests are what leads to salvation and exaltation, as is the case with Christ our Lord and Saviour (2: 1 - 4). To do this they have to have the mind of Christ Jesus, their supreme example of humility and self-sacrifice for the benefit of others, who though God, gave up that position, humbled himself by becoming a human being and even a slave and died the most humiliating death to save humankind. However, he arose from the dead and now is exalted at the right hand of the Father (2: 5 - 11). Timothy and Epaphroditus, whom Paul sends ahead of him in anticipation of his release, are commended to them. They should hold such people of God with high esteem (2: 19 - 30).

This is important for Paul because it all ties in with what working together in the gospel actually is. By starting with what he was going through, it helps them to know that they and he were sharing in the same kind of suffering and for the same reason, the gospel of Jesus Christ in which they are partners. In his case, his imprisonment has turned out to be progress for the gospel in Rome's corridors of power and a source of encouragement to his fellow preachers to get on with fearlessly preaching the gospel. Paul expects similar results when he comes to urge them to be steadfast and united, refusing to be intimidated by their opponents knowing that their salvation is in view. The sorrow they feel about his imprisonment would turn into praise and thanksgiving to God and renewed confidence and faith in God to face their opponents and live corporately in harmony with the teaching of the gospel. Thus, Paul shares his experience in prison, not just because of the Philippian church's concern about his current imprisonment, but also because he wants to use that imprisonment to shape their understanding of what partnership in the gospel entails, especially in the midst of suffering they are going through. By starting with his own experience and understanding of what he is going through, Paul brings out other practical examples of what it takes to be partners in the gospel, thus helping them to steadfastly live out their lives according to the gospel. Therefore, in making the choice to start with his experience in prison, Paul was not simply giving a "biographical prologue" before he begins work on the body of his letter from 1: 27, as scholars like Robert Swift say.

Advancing the Gospel in the midst of suffering, 1: 12 - 18

[12]I will want you to know brothers, that my circumstances have led more into the progress of the gospel. [13]that my imprisonment for the sake of Christ has become clear to the whole government officials and all the rest. [14]and the majority of the brothers in the Lord who were persuaded by my imprisonment dare to speak the word far more without fear.

[15]Some proclaim the gospel out of envy and rivalry while others proclaim Christ through good will [16]the latter out of love, having known that I have been put here in defence of the gospel. [17]Whether they are proclaiming Christ from selfish ambition, or pure motives, thinking to stir up my imprisonment, [18]what does it matter? Provided that in one way or another, whether under false motives or right motives, Christ is proclaimed. In this I also rejoice and I will rejoice again.

A leader who knows his calling and has a vision for his calling is never deterred from carrying out that calling to the letter no matter what stands in his way of doing so. Such a leader is not only in control and knows where he is going, but knows the sufferings and associated issues, and uses all the godly means at his disposal to undo those sufferings for the betterment of the people he leads and to the honour and glory of God who called him to the ministry of the gospel. He is so intimately attached to his people that he understands their suffering in the light of his own suffering; that their suffering is for the cause of the gospel of Jesus Christ as is his own. Moreover, he sees that their suffering and the cause of the gospel are far greater than his own welfare and security. He is, therefore, not so much concerned about his critics as he is about the plight of the people he leads.

This is the challenge Paul, Timothy, Epaphroditus and above all, our Lord Jesus Christ leave for Christian leaders to emulate today. The sufferings of Paul, the Philippian church and above all, of Jesus Christ, all advanced the cause of the gospel and of God the Father. This is an extremely important lesson the church today must learn as it seeks to survive her own suffering in the midst of unchecked terrorism from religious extremists whose actions governments and security agencies seem powerless to defeat.

Paul opens the body of the letter and the issue of their suffering at the hands of their opponents with his own story of imprisonment, not only because he is concerned about his situation, but also because his story sets the pace for dealing with their own story of suffering. Both his story, and theirs, belong to the same suffering and from the same opponents. He comforts them by telling them that his imprisonment, instead of ruining the gospel, has rather brought progress to it, for it has enabled the Praetorian Guards or Palace Guards to know that he is in prison for the cause of the faith and not for crime committed on his part. Furthermore, it has also encouraged preachers to preach zealously and fearlessly (vv. 12-14). He tells them that even though some preach with good will and others with selfish ambitions, this does not matter as long as Christ is preached. It is in this that he continues to rejoice (vv. 18).

Verse 12 thus makes the transition from the address to the first subject matter in the body of the letter by Paul's usual transition formula, "I want you to know, brothers." In I Corinthians he uses the transition formula, "I appeal to you, brothers"[3] (I Cor. 1: 10), to move from thanksgiving to the body of the letter. In 2 Corinthians, he uses, "We do not want you to be ignorant, brothers"[4](1: 8). He wants them to know that his imprisonment has led to more progress in the gospel instead of slowing it down or impeding it. Verses 13 and 14 give proof of this progress. The imprisonment has enabled the Pretorian Guards to come to a clearer understanding of why he is in prison, not for a crime he has committed but rather because of his faith and the gospel of Christ that he preaches. Within the church, the majority of the brethren in the Lord who believed he was being persecuted for the gospel, now dare to preach the gospel even more fearlessly. Since the Philippians were his partners in the gospel and have been worried about his imprisonment, Paul wants to let them know that his imprisonment has advanced the gospel cause. They should rejoice that the gospel has advanced right into the emperor's palace. Joseph A. Marchal, rightly notes Paul's grouping of the people into their different associations in this verse and the verses that follow because of his desire for a certain kind of community.[5] Here he talks of "the whole praetorian guards" and "all the rest" in v. 13. Paul evidently enjoyed good relations with the soldiers in the palace. Based on his greetings from Caesar's household at the end of the letter it seems that some of them did become Christians (4: 22). This helps readers understand why Paul starts with his experience in prison. He has not been at it alone. God himself has been with him in his own business. Indeed, the Philippian church was in that same business with him for they had sent Epaphroditus and material help to assist him, as they had been doing until the opportunity was blocked. They had continued in that

---

[3]παρακαλωδευμαας, αδελφος.
[4]Οθγαρθελομενυμαςαγνονοειν.
[5]Joseph A. Marshall, p. 125.

material aspect of the partnership even though other churches did not. So, even in the telling his own story, their partnership in the gospel, their consideration for the interest of others and their sharing in each other's riches and wants is made vividly clear here.

In v. 14, Paul goes on to say that it is not only that the palace guards and others have come to know that he is in prison for his faith and not for any crime. His imprisonment has encouraged the majority of his fellow preachers to rise up to the challenge of preaching the gospel fearlessly, far more than ever before. His courage in standing for the gospel at all cost persuaded them too to preach the gospel without fear of intimidation or death. By so doing, they supplement his preaching ministry in his absence. Thus, he may be in chains, but the gospel has not been chained, because God has turned his imprisonment into its progress.

Thus, as Paul says in Romans 8: 28, "And we know that in all things God works for the good of those who love him, who have been called according to his purpose." This is precisely what Paul is saying here in Philippians 1: 12 - 26, regarding his imprisonment. Although this has made him anxious as to whether he would live or be executed, he says that the imprisonment has become a great witness of the gospel to the whole palace guard and to others. Not only that, it has encouraged the majority of the believers around to rise up to preaching the gospel with zeal and without fear of intimidation.

However, he makes it clear in v. 15 that these preachers who have been persuaded to preach the gospel fearlessly in his absence, are in two categories; those doing it out of envy and rivalry and those doing it out of good will. Like rival philosophers or their students, those preachers of the gospel preaching Christ out of envy and rivalry toward Paul felt they were in competition with Paul, as is sometimes the case among some pastors today. What are their grudges against Paul? Paul does not tell us, because his interest is in the fact of their preaching Jesus Christ crucified and not their injury to his person. Verse 16 says that the second category of preachers preach Christ out of love for Paul, knowing (*oi̇otes*) that he is in prison in defence of the gospel. Thus, they are not supporting Paul out of emotions, but out of knowledge and understanding of what Paul is into and why he is in prison.

On the other hand, the fearless preaching of the others was hypocritical and full of insincerity because it was being motivated by personal or selfish ambition. This selfish ambition arose out of envy and rivalry against Paul himself. In v. 17 he gives the grounds for their envy and rivalry. He says that those who preach out of selfish ambition were "thinking to stir up my imprisonment." This was most likely because, in contrast to the preachers who supported Paul, they did not believe in his innocence. This may explain why Paul does not condemn them or denounce their proclamation of Christ, because Paul himself, not preaching Christ was their problem. This group thought by preaching out of envy and rivalry against Paul that they would make his situation in prison worse with the authorities.

They proclaim Christ from motives of selfish ambition because an arrogant spirit of self-seeking grips them. Significantly, the perspective of this group is different: While the first *'know'* that Paul has been appointed by God for the defence of the gospel and interpreted correctly the meaning of his captivity, the second group *'suppose'* that through their preaching they will stir up trouble for Paul as a prisoner.[6]

Thus, they believed Jesus Christ and preached his gospel but had no confidence in Paul. Their problem was their own selfish passions and desires, which obstructed their understanding of the grounds for Paul's imprisonment. And his imprisonment appeared to have given them the opportunity to take advantage over him to gain popularity

---

[6]O'Brien, p. 101.

for themselves. By undermining the person of Paul, they thought they would spoil Paul's case and they would have a field day in the preaching ministry. However, Paul says, that instead his imprisonment has boosted the gospel. As such, their envy against Paul did not change his vision. Their envy or selfish ambition did not make him defensive, or to ridicule those envious preachers or forget the purpose of his calling. Instead, he responded positively in v. 18 saying, "What does it matter?" The answer of this would be, "It does not matter at all, provided in one way or the other Christ's name is proclaimed." Thus, since the imprisonment made it possible for him to share the good news of salvation with the palace guards, and it also enabled his fellow preachers to supplement his preaching with much more zeal in his absence, Paul was satisfied. Since people are being won for Christ, and believers are being strengthened by their preaching, he would not see those who took advantage of his imprisonment as his enemies. Verse 18 says that they were not only out to make names for themselves, but also were out to ruin the personality of Paul. The imprisonment was a good opportunity for them to do this. Since he would not be there to respond but only hear that they have taken over and in a way that his person was being attacked, they thought he would become frustrated. However, Paul's response was a surprise, not only to his antagonists, but also to everyone including us today. For Paul was primarily focused on the gospel, his name or his person was not a big deal. Moreover, since they all preached Christ, whether from false or sincere motives, this was not an issue for Paul. Paul rejoiced that they had been given the opportunity to preach the gospel fearlessly, because the gospel was being championed in his absence. The repetition in the verse, "In this I also rejoice and I will rejoice again," is to stress the point that he is excited at this, even though some do it for the wrong reason. This can only come from someone who truly knows what partnership in the gospel entails and is wholly committed to it. Others for whom the gospel is not a priority, but rather fulfilling their personal ambition, will have all the time to waste in rivalry and baseless competitions for personal popularity and positions of honour and financial gain. Such persons will not mind tearing apart the unity and integrity of the church to achieve their selfish ambitions.

One of the things that blocks the church being effective across the globe today is competition and rivalry for status, popularity and positions of leadership in the church and the larger society, both in the church and outside it. These competitions are but visible marks of false belief and lack of understanding that no preacher or church can truly take the place of another or deprive another of his or her rightful place in the scheme of God in his church. However, he who is secure in his or her position in Christ is not shaken by such selfish ambition manifested in rivalry and envy against a believer. Indeed, such competitions and rivalry are childish, as Paul demonstrates elaborately, for instance in I Corinthians 1: 10 - 4: 21. Not only that, people who face suffering from both fellow believers and non-believers for standing firm in the truth of the gospel, see this as fertile ground for the gospel to take its foothold in that environment. Such persons would say with the apostle Paul that whatever happens in the cause of the gospel is hallelujah, as he says in vv. 19-26.

Praising God in every circumstance, vv. 19-26

[19]For I know that this will result in my release through your prayers and the support of the spirit of Jesus Christ. [20] My earnest expectation and wish is that I will in no way be put to shame, but in all boldness as always and now, Christ will be magnified in my body, either through being alive or through

> death. [21] For me, to be alive is Christ and to die is gain. [22]So, if it means living in the flesh, this to me is fruitful labour. Which shall I choose? I do not know. [23]So, I am caught up between the two. I have the passion to die and be with Christ, which is by far better. [24]But to remain in the physical body is very necessary for you. [25]And confident of this, I know that I will remain and stay with you for your progress and joy [which is derived] from faith, [26]in order that the grounds of your boasting in Christ Jesus may be beyond measure in me with my coming again to you.

In these days, there is a lot of enthusiasm for the work of the gospel, especially in Africa and other majority developing nations. Not only are Christians in these nations anxious for the gospel but despite hard conditions they cooperate to carry the gospel to distant lands. Yet despite such demands for labourers for the harvest, dedicated evangelists, missionaries and pastors are more anxious to leave the work and be in heaven with their Lord. For the apostle, the choice was not so easy, and was not due to uncertainty about his salvation or his relationship with his Lord. Paul was torn between departing to be with the Lord, and remaining on earth to continue with the preaching of the gospel to unbelievers and encouraging believers to remain steadfast until the Lord's return. He chose the latter, as he was more concerned with the salvation of unbelievers and the need to strengthen believers in the faith than with his own personal rest with the Lord in heaven.

Based on what we have seen previously, and what we will see in the following verses, the desire to resign from our responsibilities on earth to be with the Lord, is not a mark of true spirituality but of a lack of true spirituality. This sometimes is often evident in the lack of seriousness in fulfilling one's God-given given responsibilities. The amount of time we devote to envying and rivalling one another as believers whether at individual, denominational or interdenominational levels is also proof that we are far more motivated by selfish ambition in the work of the gospel than we are in the real sense of it. For the apostle Paul, the test of the seriousness of his partnership with the Christians in Philippi is the difficult choice between being alive to serve them or dying to be with the Lord and have his personal rest. The reason for his indecision between the two was not due to his fear of death or desire to enjoy this world, but rather if, despite the difficult circumstances he faced, the Philippian, and other churches he had had founded, continued to need his services to the Philippians. Often those who desire to die and be with the Lord, do so partly to escape hard responsibilities in this world, both in the service of the Lord as well as in the service of humanity. We find ourselves in an era of individualistic prospects in almost all that we do, even in the church that is communal in nature, which seeks after the common good of the body or community.

Therefore, Paul in v. 19, in a positive note, goes on to state the grounds for his rejoicing in spite of his imprisonment. He rejoices because of their prayer support for his release and for the support of the Holy Spirit. He rejoices also because he knows that in the end his salvation is sure and certain, whether he is released from prison, or he is condemned to death. By the use of salvation here, Paul is probably not talking of release from prison, but salvation at the return of Christ, because of his uncertainty about his release in the verses that follow. However, he may be thinking of both, since he believed that their prayers would be answered.

This is made clear in v. 20 where he says that his earnest desire is not to be ashamed, but that he will be courageous in exalting Christ, whether alive or dead. Paul is open to the possibility that his desire and their prayers for his release may not be granted (see vv. 21 and 22). He may not be released but face death instead. These are possibilities, not because he lacks faith that their prayers would be positively answered, but for two reasons. First, as Efrain observes, Paul is aware of the serious threat his preaching is causing to the political beliefs of the Roman Empire. Paul's concepts of *euaggelion* (good news), *kurios* (Lord), *pistis* (faith), *dikaiosune* (justice) and *eirene* (peace) and others, were contrary to what the Roman authorities and even the general Roman public thought. Paul's use of these terms in relation to a rule higher than that of the Empire or Emperor was bound to be seen as treason.[7] Second, for him to be released and remain alive, is Christ and to die, is gain. So, leaving it open is neither lack of faith nor fear of death on his part. Rather he is saying that if the imprisonment leads to death, it is gain for him personally for he will rest from his labours to be with Christ in eternity, and if he is released to be alive, that is gain for Christ. Verse 22 explains what the gain is for Christ by his being alive. If he remains alive, he will continue the work of the gospel, in which he and the Philippians are partners. The verse ends without a clear choice between the two, namely, to go by what is personal gain or by what is gain for Christ. So, in v. 23, he admits his confusion over the two options open to him, for within him he desires to die and be with Christ, which for him personally is by far better. It is better for him personally because he will rest from this body and from the hardship of life. However, the other side of him says that he needs to remain alive for the sake of the Philippians (v. 24). From a personal point of view, he would prefer to die and be with Christ, but for the sake of the believing Philippian community, he would opt not to die. For Paul, therefore, the believing community's interests and wishes outweighs his own individual and personal interest of dying and being with Christ. This is not because it is wrong to have personal interests, but because the interests of the believing individual is always protected

---

[7]Afrain Agosto, pp. 285f.

within the believing community's interests. He makes this clear in his analogy of the organs of the body illustrating the importance of spiritual gifts given to every church member. Thus, in the words of J. A. Marchal, "Paul sacrifices the chance to be with Christ in order to remain for the Philippian community's benefit, demonstrating the worth of Paul's actions and the community's benefits (for which he acted)." However, left to his own desires, Paul would prefer to die.[8]

Our worth is not found in guarding our personal interest or selfish ambition but rather in the protection and defence of the interests of others in our communities and nations, no matter the cost. Jesus himself has given us an example to follow and so does Paul. This, therefore, is not impossible as often supposed. It has been proven to be possible even in our secular society by the awards given to people who have stood in defence of others rather than themselves. We should not, therefore, dismiss this simply because it is not present in some of our Christian communities. If it is not, it may simply mean that we are not living in partnership or we are not living as the church of God. Paul was convinced he would be released in order to continue with the work of the gospel among the Philippians. Through his being with them, their grounds of "rejoicing in Christ Jesus may be beyond measure." In this way, Paul does not see the suffering he and the Christians were passing through as something to mourn about, but something to rejoice about because they were partnering with Christ in his suffering. However, many Christians these days do not want to see suffering as something to rejoice in because it is partnering in Christ's suffering, and so they do all they can to rid themselves of any form of suffering, even bribing their way out of their difficult situation.

However, the apostle Paul suffered at the hands of the state, Jews and fellow preachers, as we have seen, yet he remained focused and

---

[8]J. A. Marshall p. 128; Fowl, p. 56, citing Cicero, *Ad Quintum Fratrem*, 1: 3 - 6.

even used such ugly circumstances to champion the cause of the gospel. This remains our cherished example, apart from that of the Lord Jesus himself, whom Paul sees as the true example worthy of emulation, (see 2: 5ff). Because he is going through this suffering, he has earned the right to speak to the Philippians regarding the suffering they are passing through. They are already well aware that what he has told them and what he will tell them arises from what he has gone through and is going through. Yet Paul is not discouraged; instead he is filled with joy and praise to God for what he is doing in spite of the hardships and opposition (1: 12 - 26). However, Paul doesn't contradict what he has already said by calling upon them to look up to him as their real example. Instead, he calls on them to look up to Christ Jesus, the centre of the gospel (1: 27 – 2: 30). Nevertheless, before looking up to Jesus, they would first have to know what living in partnership in the gospel entails, especially when facing external opposition.

Having successfully showed them how his imprisonment has turned out to be progress for the gospel, he is now in a position to encourage the Philippian Christians in their own suffering as a people at the hands of their opponents. To do so, he is going to call them to live their lives only as citizens of the gospel, to be steadfast at it, to be single-minded, to be of one spirit (1: 27 - 30), humble, self-sacrificial, and not selfish, for they must be like their Lord and Saviour, Jesus Christ (2: 1 - 11). In short, they have to work out their salvation as a community of the gospel, not as independent individuals. Further, they should not think that somebody out there like the government or the political leader will take them to the Promised Land. What is more, they have their sons of the soil, Timothy and Epaphroditus, who are highly dedicated to this and have gone this way with them and their partner Paul. These two have risked their lives for this gospel and are still determined to move on, united with Paul until they all achieve the salvation promised. Their testimonies during their visits to the Philippians will confirm to them that the way of salvation is the way of internal unity, steadfastness, humility, and self-sacrifice. Consideration for the interests of others in the body are indeed, the way to the salvation that is theirs in Christ Jesus, even in the midst of external oppositions (2: 19 - 30).

Spiritual power, 1: 27 - 2: 4

[27]Conduct your community life only according to the gospel of Christ, so that whether I come and see you or I hear about you, that you stand firm in one spirit, fighting together with one soul in the faith of the gospel. [28]and do not be frightened in any way by opponents. Their utter destruction is evident and your salvation is evident, and this is from God. [29]that it may be granted in you for the sake of Christ not only to believe but also to suffer on his behalf.[30]Having the same struggle, as you know I had and now hear I am having.

2.[1]Therefore, if there is any encouragement in Christ, if there is any consolation of love, if there is any partnership of the Spirit, if there is any compassion and mercy, [2]so that you may complete my joy by thinking the same way, having the same love, united in the Spirit, live in harmony with one another. [3]Do nothing on the basis of selfish ambition nor on the basis of pride, but in humility consider others better than your own interest. [4]Each of you should not look out to his own interest, but also to the interests of each and every one.

Having thus comforted them by saying his imprisonment has turned out to promote the gospel, Paul now in v. 27 takes up the issue of the suffering of the Philippian Christians, which he says in v. 30 is the same suffering as his own. Now that they heard how his own plight has turned out to be for the good of the gospel, having himself stood firm without being ashamed of the gospel, he is in a position to speak passionately and convincingly concerning their own suffering for the same reason. In vv. 27-30, he tells them that the way to withstand suffering is not by doing it alone, but by working at it together as a believing community. Moreover, the way to do so as a community is to conduct or live their lives as a united people in Christ, not of Philippi or of Rome, but of the gospel or of heaven. They are to be steadfast in doing so, fighting suffering together in one spirit, having the same mind and being unmindful of the opposition from their opponents. 2: 1 - 4 pick up the issue of how this communal life worthy of the gospel is to be carried out.[9]

First, he says, "Conduct your community life only according to the gospel of Christ." Paul's use of *politeusthe (community life or citizen life)* is critical in understanding what he is telling the Philippian Church. The use of this significant word in Greco-Roman politics is a matter of debate among biblical scholars. Some say that Paul is calling on them to conduct themselves in line with the politics of the city of Philippi, of which some of the believers are citizens. There is difficulty with this understanding because it is not in line with the first part of the verse, talk less of the verses that follow. The kind of behaviour he is asking them to have is one that is only in accordance with the gospel of Christ. He is using *politeuein* in the sense of living a community life that is in line solely with the gospel of Christ and not in line with the general life of the city's citizenry. In other words, they are a citizenship with its own distinct sets of lifestyles and politics, different from the citizenship of Rome or of Philippi, whose lifestyles and politics are contrary to that of the gospel or of God.

This statement automatically puts the Christians in Philippi in opposition to the rest of the people of the city and the Roman

---

[9]See. S. E. Fowl, pp. 78ff.

authorities. Someone who was solely a citizen of Rome or Philippi worshiped the Emperor and other gods and followed other customs that were contrary to the Christian faith. Christians however, while obeying all other Roman laws and customs that were not contrary to the Christian faith, worshipped only God through Christ Jesus.

Maybe this is where the difficulty comes for some Nigerian scholars who believe that government and Christianity are synonymous. However, such scholars have failed to realize that this is not what is on ground. This is not what obtains in the corridors of power in Washington, London, Abuja, Paris, Accra, etc. In the corridors of power in the US, for example, strict laws on the separation of church and state greatly restrict any religious influences on the government. By contrast, in Roman corridors of power, Emperor-worship and worship of gods was encouraged even though Christianity, because of the lifestyle of its worshippers and worship of a different God and Lord, was rejected. Even in the political corridors of power in Europe or in Africa, where Christianity still has some nominal influence, total loyalty to the powers that be, is not shared with God. Authoritarian leaders often regard themselves as like a god whose words are always final and who treat contrary views as treason. Elsewhere, the worship of God is only a lip service or a religious gimmick for public consumption in a country where either a religion is very strong or state religions/churches remain entrenched in prominent positions.

Thus, the Philippian Christians faced hardship because they were living different lives to the unbelieving Philippians and the authorities. As far as the Philippian unbelievers were concerned, the Christian life was offensive. Yet Paul, instead of telling the Christians in Philippi to live as the Romans, writes to encourage them to be different, to live as a community of believers or of the gospel only, not as people with dual citizenship or lifestyle of this world and of heaven. Even in the midst of suffering from the hands of their opponents, they must only conduct their lives in accordance with the gospel, whose citizens they are.

This was like adding fuel to the fire, something that some of the Philippian Christians must have found difficult to swallow, especially those who were citizens and government workers, who must render loyalty to Rome for the privilege of citizenship and employment. Furthermore, the governing authorities and the non-believing citizens would have seen Paul's teaching as direct opposition to the order of the day. Rome saw this kind of religious teaching as treasonous, very dangerous to the political stability of the Empire, just as today any liberationist's advocacy is often thought to be anti-government propaganda that must be swiftly dealt with by governments.[10] It appears that Paul emphasized this distinct way of living the Christian life right from the beginning of his ministry in Philippi. We see this opposition to Paul's distinction between the communities of faith and un-faith, whether in Philippi or elsewhere, right at the inception of the gospel in Philippi in Acts 16: 20f. Here the owners of a slave girl testified before the city authorities against Paul and Silas, saying, "These men are Jews, and are throwing our city into an uproar by advocating customs unlawful for us Romans to accept or practice" (NIV). M. Bockmuehl is thus right when he says:

> Acts 16: 20f suggests that Paul's mission was perceived to be just such a menace to the integrity of the Philippian polity and citizenship, and it is easy to see why the same sorts of people would perceive the ensuing Pauline church to present the same sort of threat: Christians who explicitly defined their citizenship . . . and their locus of supreme sovereignty (2: 9 -

---

[10]Bockmuehl, p. 100.

> 11) to be elsewhere, must necessarily incur the odium of being
> 'un-Roman' enemies of the public order.[11]

Therefore, we are dealing with an external opposition here, the governing authorities and other unbelievers within the city and not an internal opposition within the Philippian church. The external opposition the Philippian Christians are facing is thus the same external opposition Paul himself is facing and for the same cause, that is the gospel and what it teaches (1: 30), distinct from Roman beliefs and teaching.

Thus, Paul used his Roman citizenship only whenever he felt it necessary, especially to enhance the gospel. He never behaved or lived his life as a Roman citizen. Rather, he conducted his life as a citizen of heaven, the reason for which he was in prison. By saying that they should conduct their community life only in accordance with the gospel of Christ, he is saying here that they should follow the way of life he has taken. However, as he says in Romans 13: 1 - 6, Paul is not disregarding Roman law or that the Christian should not obey the laws of his country, since he says that obedience to such laws is sanctioned by God as long as they are they do not go against God or make us deny God. In the light of this, we have to say that such laws must be followed unless they undermine God or our faith in God.

The remaining part of v. 27 goes on to say, "so that whether I come and see you or I hear about you, that you stand firm in one spirit, fighting together with one soul in the faith of the gospel." Living differently as a believing community from the larger community is a difficult thing that demands a lot from the believer. Here, Paul says it demands standing firm in one spirit. It demands struggling together with one or the same mind in the faith of the gospel and not each one

---

[11]Ibid. pp. 100f.

for himself or herself. To live differently from the rest of society around them demands that the believers live and act in accordance with the gospel and not individually, as one sees fit, independent of each other, but as a body. Secondly, as they live as one united body or community of believers and not individually, they are to stand firm, to be steady, consistent or unyielding in their faith and not to be unstable in the way they live as Christians. Thirdly, as they stand firm together in a faith that is rooted in the gospel, they are to see that they make it to the end, even in the midst of the trying times they are experiencing.[12] Thus, what they are and everything they do has to be gospel-based, if their unity and steadfastness is going to yield the fruit of salvation that is theirs (1: 28).

The third thing they are to do as a believing community is mentioned in v. 28. They are not to be "frightened in anyway by their opponents," but are to be brave and courageous, living their lives in the city without fear of intimidation. Intimidation and creating fear in people are often ways that governing authorities use against their own citizens to ensure obedience. Scholars debate what the next part of the verse means. It is hard to understand what Paul means by saying that the destruction of the opponents will be evident and their own salvation would be apparent when, as Christians, they stand firm as one indivisible body. Is Paul talking of the opponents' imminent physical destruction? If so, who will destroy them? Not the Christians of course! Moreover, in what way will the salvation of the Christians be evident? Will it be through some miraculous work of God or repentance on the part of the opponents after their physical destruction?

The difficulty with this view makes other scholars think that the phrase refers to the salvation of Christians and the destruction of opponents of the gospel at Christ's return. This is unlikely. Note that

---

[12]See Markus Bockmuehl, p. 99.

the last phrase of the verse says, "And this is from God." As Bockmuehl notes, it looks like both destruction and salvation are to take place both now and at Christ's return. The unwavering unity of Christians and the inability of the governing authorities to stop the gospel from progressing means defeat for the authorities, proving the certainty of the destruction of the unbelievers at the return of Christ, because God is the one who is always in control. However, Paul and the Christians in Philippi could see this.[13] The authorities simply saw the Philippians' resistance as stubbornness that yielded no good results, since they had to face the wrath of the authorities. They knew the Christians could do nothing against the Roman authorities except flee to save their lives. Further, the authorities believed the Christians would eventually be caught as the eye of Rome was everywhere in the empire. While the Roman authorities felt threatened by the Christian religion, they always felt that they could crush the Christians whenever they desired. Yet as Paul shows from his own experience, the Philippian Christians should realise that their suffering was not a mark of defeat or of their imminent destruction but a necessary share in the suffering of Jesus that Christians have to experience (v. 29). Hence, his advocating for steadfastness, unity, and struggling together with one mind and spirit. Verse 30 says, therefore, that he and they are in the same suffering. What they are going through is what he has been going through and is now going through and yet he is not discouraged in any way, because the victory is his and so it is theirs as well. They only need to work at it together with perseverance and not individually.

As has been indicated, 2: 1 - 4 go on to talk of how this common life of the believing community is to be lived, especially in the midst of suffering, and what it entails. Verse 1 lists four values expected of everyone in the community, if the community is to be steadfast, able

---

[13]Bockmuehl, p. 101.

to stand firm in one spirit and able to fight together with one soul and mind in the faith of the gospel. These four values are necessary for this spirit of communal living or "common" living, to use Fowl's term. The use of "if", here does not make what is said about the four values conditional, as some may suppose. These values, which were to be imbibed by each member of the believing community are: encouragement in Christ, consolation of love, partnership of the Spirit and compassion and mercy. When Paul says in v. 2 that they should make his joy complete by being of the same mind and soul on these, he is not saying that he has not exhibited these values, but because he has exhibited these, he wants them all to agree or have the same mind regarding these values. Thus, Paul is not making a conditional statement by using the "if" but he is using it to express an affirmative action that he has demonstrated to their notice. He means to say that he had made encouragement and not commands and this encouragement had been in Christ, or in accordance with the gospel teaching and not in oneself.

The remaining words or values take the genitive, "of love," "of Spirit," which should be understood as genitive of possession except the last two words, "compassion" and "mercy." That is, his consolation has been that which is rooted in his love for them. And his partnership with them in the gospel has not been the societal partnerships common in Greco-Roman society, but is a partnership which belongs to the Holy Spirit or is derived from the Holy Spirit. This is because wherever the word, *koinonia*, is followed by the genitive, it is be understood as possessive genitive.[14] Moreover, he has shown them a heart of compassion and mercy. A careful look at the words, encouragement, consolation, partnership, compassion and mercy reveals that they are closely related in that they are words that make unity possible in a

---

[14]P. Yamsat 1992. ....

society or community.[15] The appeal in v. 2 confirms this affirmative response, for v. 2 says that in doing so, they would complete his joy by thinking in the same direction, having the same love, united in the Spirit and living in harmony with one another. They are not to do anything "on the basis of selfish ambition nor on the basis of pride, but in humility," they are to consider others better than their own interests. Each of them should not look out for his or her interest only, but should look out for each other's interests. It is by so doing that both the individual and the community would be saved. Salvation cannot be achieved by each person struggling independently to defend and serve his or her own interest, for as the slogan goes, "divided we fall, but united we stand." For Paul therefore, this suffering they are undergoing cannot lead to a life of survival of the fittest. The suffering instead should create a lifestyle that is communally centred, which in a way is a Christian citizenship life that is in line with the gospel, (cf. 1: 27). Those who possess the citizenship of Philippi are loyal to Rome and the Emperor, but those who belong to the Christian citizenship of the gospel in Philippi are loyal to Christ. Those who belong to the citizenship of the city of Philippi are status prone, self-serving and individualistic, competing against each other for status, but those who belong to the Christian citizenship in Philippi use their status for the benefit of the rest of the citizens. They are thus, community conscious, self-sacrificial, protecting and defending one another's interests instead of competing over interests or any available openings.

These ways of relating to each other are spelt out in 2: 2b - 4, both in the positive and negative. Positively, they are to think the same way or as Fowl puts it, have the same pattern of thinking, having the same love, united in the spirit, living in harmony with one another, considering others and their interests better than one's own interest

---

[15]Fowl, p. 79, p. 81f.

and thus, protecting and defending the interests of each and every one in the community. Verse 3 expresses the negative behaviour to be avoided in community relationships, behaviour found to be common in non-Christian citizenship relationship. These are selfish ambition, pride and self-interest. As Fowl observes, they are "to hold the same perspective by seeing things the same way," which will generate and give direction to a particular course of action, like standing firm and being like-minded.[16]

It needs to be observed here even though this kind of political language was central in Greco-Roman politics of concord and friendship; it was in a way different, as already stated in 1: 27, by the use of the word "only." To Paul's Greco-Roman contemporaries, this was an odd kind of political concord and friendship, because it seeks the welfare or interest of others instead of one's own interest. As Fowl observes, it was not only odd as far as Greco-Roman politicians were concerned, it undermined the imperial political culture.[17]

Thus, while 1: 27 - 30 is saying that the salvation of the Philippians even in the midst of suffering lies in unity through steadfastly struggling together with one mind and spirit, 2: 1 - 4 goes further. Unity, which is simply to fight an external opponent, cannot bring the lasting salvation in view. There must be internal cohesion, indebtedness to one another as citizens of the same gospel, each person his/her brother's/sister's keeper, roots in Christianity in the leadership of the Holy Spirit and not reliance on human might and power.

Before bringing Timothy and Epaphroditus into the discussion in order to show the Philippians that he is not alone in this way of thinking, Paul brings in Jesus and his way of life to strengthen what he has been saying. Jesus has been at the centre of all this talk right from

---

[16]Fowl, p. 82.
[17]Fowl, p. 87.

the beginning of the letter. Paul is bringing in the life of Jesus Christ before that of Timothy and Epraphroditus not merely as an example but as the Chief Citizen of this Christian citizenry upon whom every Christian conduct is to be patterned.

Having the mind of Christ, 2: 5 - 11

> [5]Have this same mind in you, as it was also in Christ Jesus. [6]Who being in the form of God, did not take equality with God something to be grasped, [7]being born in the likeness of a man; and having been found in appearance as a man, [8]He humbled himself, becoming obedient to the point of death and of death on the cross. [9]Therefore God has exalted him and granted him the name above every name, [10]that at the name of Jesus, every knee of the heavens and of the earth and under the earth should bow, [11]and every tongue confess that Jesus Christ is Lord, to the glory of God the Father.

Since their common life is to be ordered according to their heavenly citizenship, because their loyalty is to Christ in whose gospel they are partners, their lifestyle also has to be patterned according to the life of Christ. Thus, they should have the mind of Christ. In 2: 5 - 11, Jesus Christ is, therefore, brought into this discussion of how the Philippians are to corporately behave in the midst of suffering, in order to support what Paul has been teaching...

Having tried to show them that unity and self-denial are needed to resist their external opponents, he calls on them to note that this was the mind of Jesus Christ, a mind that was clothed in humility and self-sacrifice in the face of suffering. Yet in the end, he won the day. He was exalted! Thus, suffering for the sake of others, a life of humility and self-sacrifice does not mean defeat but is a means to victory. For them, as for Jesus Christ, it is the path to victory and exaltation. The Philippians should, therefore, have the mind of Christ, in whose gospel they are partners with one another and with Paul through Christ in the gospel.

What was the mind of Christ? Verse 6 acknowledges that Jesus Christ was in the form of God before coming to earth, but that Jesus did not believe that divine form was something for him to tenaciously hold onto in competition with God the Father. Rather, Jesus was willing to let it go for the good of and for the salvation of humankind. Yet some Christian political leaders, compete for exalted secular positions of authority and, if gained, refuse to relinquish them when their term of office expires, even if a change of leadership would be for the good of the people. In some countries they may even try to change the constitution to allow them to stay in office indefinitely. Different reasons are suggested for such behaviour including being power drunk, or not wanting to be subservient to anyone coming after them or perhaps because they need to cover their tracks from any successor probing them.

Some religious leaders behave very similarly. Thus, people generally, do not want to serve or to take the lower position because they want to be served without end. They want to rise to the top above others, but not to come down below others. This is the main reason for the problems we have in many nations, especially in Africa. No one wants to serve but to be served and so there is competition and rivalry for the few positions of authority. But 2: 7, says that Jesus did not feel that divine form was something to hold on to tightly, but it is something he willingly released to become a human being through his birth as a human baby. As if becoming a human being was not a sufficient mark of humility, 2: 8 goes on to say that he humbled himself further by becoming obedient to the point of death, in particular death on the cross. Thus, he became like the worst human beings, a criminal and a slave. It is as if dying like any human being was insufficient an identification with human beings, but that he had to die the worst of deaths, of the worst of criminals, on the cross.

"What a crazy way of living!" the citizens of the city of Philippi and of Rome would say. Nevertheless, for Paul and Jesus Christ, it is in the act of dying, in releasing or giving up one's interest for others that exaltation comes. Therefore, vv. 9-11 say,

> Therefore God has exalted him and granted him the name above every name, that at the name of Jesus, every knee in the heavens and of the earth and under the earth should bow, and every tongue confess that Jesus Christ is Lord, to the glory of God the Father.

This spirit of self-sacrifice and humility that promotes unity, is something Paul wants them to imbibe as a gospel community. It is not, however, of his creation or of human origin. Rather it is from Christ Jesus, brought about by God through Christ's sacrificial work. Through Christ's work, God the Father has united himself with humanity and has united human beings with each other.

In fostering human unity, self-interest is often an obstacle. The enemy uses this desire to serve one's personal interest over and above the community's common interest. In a community where self-interest is above the common interest of the community, the community suffers defeat from the hands of its external opponents. However, the Philippian believers ought not to follow the way of life of the citizens of Rome or Philippi, where self-interest was central. Rather they should follow the way of the citizen of Christ or of heaven and the gospel, which emphasised community interests. To this they have been called and to this they belong, even in the midst of suffering. By taking up this humble and self-sacrificial mind set out by Jesus Christ himself, having a mind which puts others first and one's own interests second, they would be able to live harmoniously with one another and be able to face any external opponent successfully. Whether alive or dead, they will surely meet with the anticipated salvation, while their opponents meet the awaited destruction. This certainly calls for working out or cultivating their salvation without grudges or murmuring, since they are not at it alone but God is working with them and in them.

Work out your salvation, 2: 12 - 18

[12]Therefore, my beloved, as you have always done, not only as in my presence, but now much more in my absence; work out your salvation with fear and trembling. [13]for God is working in you also that which he wishes and effectively too.

[14]Do everything without complains and questions, [15]so that you may become blameless and pure children of God, faultless in the midst of a crooked and perverted generation, in which you shine as light in the world. [16]holding up the word of life so that I may boast in the day of Christ that I did not run empty-handed nor work in vain.[17]but if I should be poured out as a drink offering for the sacrifice and service of your faith, I rejoice and rejoice [again] with all of you. [18]And in this you also rejoice and you should still rejoice with me.

This self–sacrifice of Christ, leading to exaltation does not mean that believers should sit down, lose heart or follow the citizenship of Rome, because of either current or anticipated suffering. Rather, Christ's self-sacrifice calls for believers to work hard to bring their anticipated salvation to reality, says Paul in vv. 12-18. A united, harmonious, self-less and sacrificial life patterned after our Lord Jesus Christ demands that all of us, whether clergy or laity, live pure lives as children of God. Many preachers or spiritual leaders seem concerned only about their own salvation and wellbeing and not about the holistic welfare of believers generally. This was not so with the apostle Paul. He was so concerned about the Philippians that he instructed them to work hard to show the result of their salvation by obeying God with deep reverence and fear and to do everything they could do without grumbling and argumentation. Paul had warned the Corinthian church against the danger of returning to idolatry having tasted the goodness of the gospel. They would perish just as the children of Israel also perished in the wilderness for doing so (1 Corinthians 10: 1ff). This is the danger the Philippian church is running into, should they allow themselves to be intimidated by those who oppose their way of life, a lifestyle that completely contradicts that of the unbelieving citizens of Philippi. The children of Israel had grumbled or murmured against Moses in the wilderness and were destroyed (Numbers 14). The same too would happen to the believing Philippians if they also grumble, because God is not partial. He acts in the same way toward Christians who, out of lack of faith in him, grumble about the distinctively direction he wants his people to go in as he acts with their unbelieving contemporaries.

Paul, therefore, charged them in vv. 12-18 to hold firmly as a people to the word of God that gives life to every believer. By so doing, they would validate his work among them and his spiritual race in this world would not have been in vain. True partnership in the gospel is thus concerned about the success and salvation of all in the partnership wherever the people may be. It is not about one's individual success and salvation only, as found in the citizens of Rome or Philippi where competition and selfish ambition was the order of the day. As the Mupun of Nigeria would say, "Two is wealth, but to be alone is death." And "wealth without love and living together in peace and harmony is valueless" (*Vul a long, mishik a muut. Dang be long, nen walshak kii tong riyang kii shak, niki me kwop nii kas).*

Verse 12-18, therefore, is Paul's usual argument seeking to convince his readers about the manner in which they are to conduct their communal lives, a conduct which should only be in accordance with the gospel of Christ. The line of argument in these verses is joined with what precedes by the use of "therefore"/*hoste)* along with the intimate word of friendship or partnership, "my beloved" (*agape toi mou)* in v. 12. As his beloved, he again shares his confidence in them to work out their salvation despite his absence, as they have previously done in his presence. They are to do this with fear and trembling and not with pride and arrogance that demeans their partners. (The fear and trembling here has not to do with fear of opponents but it has to do with reverent fear of God). Verse 13 states why. They are not on their own as God is at work in them to effectively achieve that which he wishes in them. It is only right, therefore, that they live out their Christian citizenship humbly and harmoniously, always aware that the Lord has called them into that citizenship and that he is working out his purposes in them even in times of suffering.

Verse 14 gives some practical examples of what this means. First, the working out of salvation does not imply personal salvation as is often assumed. We have to take account of the context. Rather it is working steadfastly together despite suffering at the hands of opponents, resulting in the community's salvation. People who are working out their salvation with fear and trembling do not raise divisive complaints or questions against their fellow believers. By working out their liberated life with fear and trembling and without divisive behaviour, they would be blameless and pure children of God (v. 15). Blameless in this context does not mean sinless, but guiltless in the eyes of the law, which is explained in the next two phrases, "faultless in the midst of a crooked and perverted generation, in which you shine as light in the world." This is what Paul has been driving at, the need to live differently from their opponents by holding on to the word of life without being found wanting in any way whether within the church or in society. Verse 16 tells us that Paul's aim in convincing them to live their lives as citizens of the gospel has been to enable him boast in the day of Christ that he did not run empty-handed nor work in vain, but that they achieve the salvation promised them.

In vv. 17 and 18, Paul returns to what he said in 1: 19f, where he expresses his ambivalence concerning whether to choose death or life. After the ambivalence, he finally chose to live for the sake of the Philippians, for their spiritual progress. Here, in vv. 17f, Paul is still not certain about the outcome of his imprisonment. However, he is open to either option, whether it be death or release in orderto continue preaching the gospel. Nevertheless, if his case should lead to death, Paul takes it as a drink offering or sacrifice and a service for their faith. If it happens that way, it is a matter for him to rejoice about and to rejoice with all of them. He expects them also to rejoice, as his death will mean that he has successfully accomplished his mission in calling them to faith and maturity in Christ. Nevertheless, raising this possibility does not mean that his mission has finished. He is simply reminding them that the two options of death or remaining alive are still open. He only wants them to have this in mind so that he and they may not be taken by surprise by any turn of events. He therefore continues with the subject of self-sacrifice by drawing their attention to the self–sacrifice of Timothy and Epaphroditus.

Caring for the Church, 2: 19 - 30

I hope in the Lord Jesus to send Timothy to you soon in order that I also may be encouraged to hear about you. [20]For I have no one of the same feeling who will genuinely care about you. [21]For all of them seek after that which is theirs, not that which is of Jesus Christ. [22]And you know his worth, that as a son with his father; he has served with me in the gospel. [23] Because of this, therefore, I hope to send him as soon as I know my situation. [24]And I am certain that in the Lord I myself will come very soon.

[25]And I consider it necessary to send to you Epaphroditus, the brother, fellow worker and fellow soldier and also your messenger and minister regarding my necessity. [26]For he longs for all of you and he is distressed because you heard that he was sick. [27]For indeed he was sick and about to die. But God had mercy on him, and not on him only but also on me that I may not have sorrow upon sorrow. [28]I therefore have with great urgency to send him to you so that on seeing him, you may again rejoice and be relieved of sorrow. [29]Therefore receive him favourably in the Lord with all joy, and hold such [people] in high esteem, [30]for he came close to the point of death for the work of Christ. He risked his life in order to meet up what was lacking in your service for me.

The role of other trusted fellow preachers of the word like Timothy and Epaphroditus cannot be ignored when discussing the trials his Philippian partners are enduring for the sake of the gospel. After all Timothy and Epaphroditus are dear to the hearts of Paul and the Philippian church and Timothy is a co-author of the letter. Paul, therefore, uses their dedication and steadfastness to emphasise his call to the Philippians to be united fighting together with the same mind and spirit in the gospel. They should not be concerned about their opponents who, although they may appear to be winning are, in fact, being destroyed. Meanwhile the believers are assured of salvation in Christ, into whose gospel and citizenship they are fellow partakers.

Therefore, in vv. 19-30, Paul informs the Philippians that he would send their close friends Timothy and Epaphroditus to them at the appropriate time. These men of God would explain his letter more fully to them. The commendations he lavishes upon Timothy and Epaphroditus are worthy of notice. He does not see the young preachers he has raised up as threats or rivals to him, but as colleagues and partners in ministry, for they would be the people to take over the work after him. The quality of our leadership and partnership in the gospel is always seen in the value each leader and believer accords to the other partners "in the partnership of Jesus Christ" to which we all have been called (I Cor. 1: 9). Paul exhibits this here by affirming Timothy and Epaphroditus who themselves lived exemplary lives.

The competition among preachers of the gospel today is so ferocious that only a very few would want to commend other preachers or recommend them to some Christian communities or churches elsewhere. Even commending those they have trained to maturity and positions of recognition in the church is a difficult thing to do. However, the number of people he has trained and raised to influential positions mark out the true leader. The leader is known for his eagerness to acknowledge the fruit of his work in others and by the good recommendation given by others concerning people that he has raised. On the other hand, in a church where there is division, competition and enmity, leaders have been known to give false recommendations, whether they be positive for those close to them or negative recommendations about those they do not like. Nor is it uncommon to find those who have been properly groomed by their teacher or leaders, turning against their teachers, because they envy the high positions their mentors occupy, doing all they can to dislodge them. This is not walking in unity, with the same mind and spirit. This is not the attitude of people belonging to the same citizenship of the gospel and of heaven, which is both advocated here by Paul, and demonstrated in the lives of Timothy and Epaphroditus. As colleagues, they have lived as colleagues indeed, following after the pattern Jesus had left for his church everywhere in the world, then and now.

Verse 19 shows that one of the reasons Paul is sending Timothy to them is that he may return to Paul with news about them, especially how they are faring in the gospel. Of course, they will hear of Paul's condition and be strengthened. Timothy is ideally suited for this task because Paul knows no one else has the same feeling of genuine care for the Philippian Christians as he does (v. 20). The rest of the workers sought after personal gains instead of Christ's. Paul knows Timothy extremely well, for he brought Timothy up in the faith right from childhood and effectively he is his son in the faith. Timothy has served Paul in the work of the gospel, as well as being a faithful minister of the gospel. It is on these bases that he is sending Timothy to them and not any other person. He will send him when he is much more certain about the situation of his imprisonment (v. 23), so that they too could get more news about Paul. Moreover, if the Lord wills and he is released from prison, he certainly would visit them, as soon as possible.

Meanwhile, in v. 25, Paul goes on to say that it is necessary now for him to return to them Epaphroditus, who is a brother, fellow worker and fellow soldier with him in the gospel and messenger and minister from the Philippians meeting Paul's needs while he was in prison. These words are no mean words but words of commendation. In v. 26, he shares with them Epaphroditus' longing for all of them and not just some among them, especially when he heard that the news of his sickness had reached them. It is so common, even today among African Christians, not to let loved ones know about their sickness or misfortune, less they become worried and restless, especially when distance and the sick person separate them or the relations cannot be reached so easily. However, when the sick one hears that the loved ones have heard about the news of the sickness of a beloved one, such a person becomes more anxious and restless too and wishes to see them to relieve them of much anxiety about the truth of one's healing.

This is what happens also in a situation where there is true love in the partnership of the gospel. Moreover, this is what vv. 27 and 28 are about. Paul himself had not sent word to them about Epaphroditus' sickness, just like Epaphroditus himself had not, except now. Paul now confirms to them that indeed Epaphroditus had been sick and close to death, but God had mercy on him and much more on Paul himself, because if he had died, he would have had double sorrow. By the use of the word "double sorrow" or "sorrow upon sorrow," Paul means that he would have had two problems to contend with. First would have been the death of Epaphroditus and secondly, Paul's own imprisonment made more difficult by the absence of someone like Epaphroditus to minister to his needs in prison. Not to mention that the Philippians would have missed him dearly. For this reason, he decided to send him to them as a matter of urgency so that they may rejoice on seeing him and Paul would be relieved of sorrow.

This is followed in vv. 29 and 30 by his plea that they should receive Epaphroditus with favourable joy and to hold him in high esteem because he almost died for the work of the gospel of Christ on their behalf. He had come to serve Paul on their behalf. He had risked his life in doing so.

What else do we expect Paul to bring up in this letter to a church so intimately attached to him, which is closely related to the external opposition that has just been dealt with? Chapters 3: 1 - 4: 9 has to do with internal opposition and strife, which Paul cannot leave out of an intimate letter like this, having seen how he passionately dealt with the external threat to the church in much detail. To this we turn to in the next unit.

Questions for further reflection and study

1. Discuss Paul's attitude towards those who were preaching from wrong motives.
2. Discuss why churches cannot unite in obedience to the command of Jesus and his word but allow themselves to be persecuted even where they are in the majority.
3. Can Christians have the mind of Christ and what do we need to have Christ's mind?
4. Can Christians work out their salvation and how?

HANDLING INTERNAL OPPOSITION AND DIVISION, 3: 1 - 4:9

The question that quickly arises from what has transpired so far is, "Was the church only troubled by external opposition and not by any internal squabble?" "Are there no clues in what we have seen so far that indicate there were some unresolved problems within the church, despite the evidence of love and partnership?" We have seen in 1: 15 - 18 that from among those who because of Paul's imprisonment rose up to preach the word fearlessly, while some were preaching out of envy with the intention to injure Paul while he was in prison. Although this may not have been very pronounced in Philippi, since it took place where Paul was imprisoned. However, at least there must have been some Christians in Philippi who did not like Paul's approach to the gospel, especially his theology of a Christian citizenship in contrast to earthly citizenship, be it of Rome and/or Philippi.

A close look at 3: 1 - 4: 9 reveals that there were indeed some internal squabbles within the church. Since Paul does not take much time on this squabble in the letter, we take it that the squabble was not as pronounced as we find in the letters to the Galatians or Corinthians. Thus, while 1: 12 - 2: 30 deals with how the church in Philippi should live their lives when facing external opposition, 3: 1 - 4: 9 is a call to the church to beware of internal squabbles. In 3: 1 - 17, he calls on them to rejoice in Christ, but at the same time to beware of some Christians he calls "dogs," "evil workers" and "mutilators." These Christians he contrasts with his own life and his elevated position in the Jewish faith, which he gave up for the sake of knowing Christ Jesus. Here, he tells the Philippians about his feeling of not having arrived yet, but that he is still pressing on to perfection, which is only possible at the return of Christ. In 3: 18 - 4: 1, he calls on them to beware of enemies of the cross who set their minds on earthly things. In 4: 2 - 3, he calls on two leaders of the church, Euodia and Syntyche, to reconcile and live in harmony. The church through one of his fellow-workers is to help them in doing this. In addition, in 4: 4 - 9, he repeatedly calls on them to rejoice in the Lord, fix their eyes on Christ and not to be anxious about anything, but to do whatever is worth doing in the Lord. In other words, Paul is saying that when a church is steadfast and united against external opposition; when it is vigilant in dealing with internal squabbles and takes time to rejoice in the Lord and worship him aright, such a church is sure to achieve the salvation that is ahead of it (1: 28). Thus, it is only when a community of the gospel jealously guards what it has and rejoices over what it has, that it will possess that salvation in full at the end (1: 28, 2: 12 - 16).

Sometimes the church is active in resisting external enemies but unmindful and incapable of dealing with internal problems. Instead, it consumes itself by fighting over leadership positions or finances. If the church is to be on top of both external and internal forces, the members of the church must work together as a body and not individually. If we are to be victorious over the external forces opposing the church; if we are to take hold of the promised salvation that is in sight, as well as rejoice that we now have a foretaste of it, we must see ourselves as one indivisible body with different gifts, to be used in building each other up. Moreover, we must caution those who would prefer to tear the church apart for their selfish and worldly gains. This again, is the message of Paul to the Philippian church in 3: 1 - 4: 9 and to the church today.

Beware of Judaisers, 3: 1 - 11

[1]At the bottom of it all, my brethren, rejoice in the Lord. To write the same thing to you for me is not wearisome, for it is also a safeguard.

[2]Beware of the dogs. Beware of the evil workers and beware of the mutilators. [3]For you are the circumcision, those who worship the Spirit of God and take pride in Christ Jesus and not those who have confidence in the flesh.

[4]Although I have also [reason] for a lot of confidence in the flesh. If there is any who is to have confidence in the flesh, I have more. [5]Circumcised on the eighth day, born out of Israel, of the tribe of Benjamin, Hebrew of Hebrews, according to the Law a Pharisee, [6]according to zeal, persecuting the church, according to righteousness based on the Law, I became blameless.

[7]But whatever was my gain; I consider these as loss through Christ. [8]On the contrary, I rather consider it to be all loss through the surpassing value of knowing Christ Jesus, my Lord, through whom everything is held together and I consider them garbage/dungs so that I will gain Christ. [9]And I find in him, not having the righteousness from the Law but the faith, which is through Christ, the righteousness from God by faith, [10]to know him and the power of his resurrection and the partnership of his sufferings, sharing in his death, [11]if somehow I may/attain the resurrection of the dead.

Paul starts this new subject with the transition formula, "At the bottom line,[1] my brethren." As said in our introduction, scholars who do not see this letter as a unit wrestle over the sense of the Greek, *loipos* used here by Paul. Although Bockmuehl acknowledges that the Greek word, *liopon* in 3: 1 is used to transit from what precedes to the next subject matter, he is still of the opinion that Paul's train of thought is interrupted after 3: 1. As such, he says 3: 1 should be seen at best as a general conclusion of 2: 19 - 30, but does not help to transit into 3: 2.[2]

But the fact that 3: 1 appears to be the opposite of what follows after 3: 1, does not render the verse to be a wrong transition from the previous subject to the next. Instead, we should ask what Paul understands by the Greek, *to loipon* in this verse and whether such phrases like, "finally," "Finally brethren" or "my brethren" was used to transit from one subject matter in other letters of Paul and in Greco-Roman letters or not. Moreover, we may even ask, is it possible for Paul to use *to loipon* here as a transition formula, even if not found elsewhere in his letters? Above all, our attention may not simply be tied to the word *loipos,* "finally" and its sense, but that our translation of this word must fit the context, fits what precedes and what follows it. This is important, because even if we were to accept that this is a composite letter, the composer must have seen a relationship between what precedes and what follows before deciding to choose to use the word, *loipos,* since we cannot assume he was a novice in writing letters. As a good writer,[3] he should have noticed that it is not the right word to use and so would have used a better word to connect to the next subject matter. However, *loipos* cannot be understood in the sense of

---

[1]Cf. O'Brien, p. 348; G. Fee, pp. 288-291

[2]Bockmuehl, p. 176f.

[3]Whether we say this was the problem of his scribe, the scribe would normally have shared what he wrote with Paul and Paul would have made the corrections.

"finally" here. As O'Brien says, it can be understood in the sense of "well then," "and so," "therefore," or "moreover."[4] Alternatively, it can be understood to mean, "at the bottom of it all."

Paul has been consistent in saying that the Philippians' salvation and the destruction of their opponents lies in their being steadfast and in struggling together with one mind and spirit in the midst of such opposition. Hence, it is right for him to call on them to rejoice in the midst of the opposition and in the midst of the dogs and mutilators from within. This, he would do, not only because of what joy can do at such a time, but more so that God is at work in them in Christ Jesus (2: 13). Moreover, rejoicing in the Lord Jesus in the midst of suffering, opposition or problems is not out of place within the body of the letter. In 1: 18 - 19, Paul had said this concerning those who were preaching Christ merely to offend his personality:

> What does it matter? Provided that in one way or another, whether under false motives or right motives, Christ is proclaimed. In this I also rejoice and I will rejoice again. For I know that through your prayers and the support of the spirit of Jesus Christ, this will result in my release.

In addition, on doing everything without complaints and questions, whether with regard to his suffering or the external opponents, he says in 2: 17 - 18,

> But if I should be poured out as a drink offering for sacrifice and the service of your faith, I rejoice and rejoice with all of you. [18]And in this you also rejoice and you should also rejoice with me.

It is, therefore, not out of place to see 3: 1 as a good closing for the preceding external opposition and transition to the internal squabbles

---

[4]O'Brien, p. 348 and Bockmuehl, "and beyond that", p. 176.

that follow, both of which are tough experiences. To use Paul's words, what he is calling them to do in 3: 1, "is a safeguard for you." What is that "safeguard", "safety measure" or "security" and a "safeguard" against what? This safeguard is the act of rejoicing in the Lord always. Realizing that he has said this several times, he apologizes for the repetition, but then he tells them that he is doing it on purpose. To call on them to rejoice repeatedly should not be seen as meaningless repetition, but something good, because to rejoice always is a safeguard against both the external opposition he has just finished talking about and against the internal problems he is going to talk about. The Christian life is much more than the struggles of life faced by the Christian. We have the Lord always to rejoice with and we have the salvation, peace and freedom he brings to us to rejoice in. When the people of God rejoice in the Lord, that act of rejoicing in the Lord gives the believer a sense of security as regards his or her salvation both now and in the future with the return of Christ, despite all of the oppositions. There is nothing more crippling than being buried in sorrow because of the problems that come one's way. Sorrow brings fear and fear destroys, but rejoicing in the Lord and in his power, in spite of all the odds, brings courage and courage brings hope and faith, and faith and hope bring victory over whatever problems that may want to swallow up the church or the individual believer. Having said this, Paul then draws the attention of the Philippians to the things that they need to beware of and avoid, whether those things are already on ground or are yet to manifest themselves in the church in Philippi.

To rejoice in the Lord is the right thing to do, or the basic thing for the Christian to do in every circumstance, rather than to be buried by opposition or problems. Time should be taken to rejoice in the Lord because rejoicing is the life and power of the church. The traditional African knows this psychology of rejoicing in the midst of suffering very well, for it is not uncommon to notice a woman resort into a series of songs while in the midst of problems or after a fight with another woman or her husband. Moreover, it is common to hear the husband join her in conversational song. Even though such songs may be expressions of the hurt, it does not lead to further fight or anger. My mother and father used to sing after a verbal rift. It is more of a reflective and therapeutic thing for both parties. Thus, as M. Bockmuehl says in his conclusion of 3:1,

> What Paul is saying in verse one, therefore, is that he does not mind repeating his call to joy in the Lord because it is this which will serve them as safeguard in every situation – including of course such external and internal threats as the rest of the letter goes on to address.[5]

O'Brien also says:

> This is not an admonition to some kind of superficial cheerfulness that closes its eyes to the surrounding circumstances.[6] Rather, the apostle is inculcating a positive Christian attitude of joy that finds outward expression in their lives and that realistically takes into account the adverse circumstances, trials, and pressures through which the Philippians were called to pass. It also recognizes God's mighty working in and through those circumstances to fulfil his own gracious purposes in Christ.[7]

Therefore, Paul in v. 2, moves straight to ask the Philippian Christians to beware of "the dogs, evil workers and mutilators." Exactly who

---

[5]Bockmuehl, p. 182.

[6]As the Stoic and Cynics used to do.

[7]O'Brien, p. 349; G. Fee, p. 291. The call to rejoice even in the midst of external opposition (1: 18; 2: 17f) and in the midst of internal problems (3: 1; 4: 1, 4 and 6) runs through the letter.

these are, has been a matter of debate among scholars. Since Paul is not interested in telling us who they are, working out who they are requires a reconstruction that will help us to understand what he is interested in telling the church in Philippi. To begin with, we need to ask whether the dogs, evil workers and mutilators here refer to three different groups of people or whether it is referring to the same group of people, but using three different terms for them. According to Psalms 22: 16, evil people are referred to as dogs. In addition, according to Rev. 22: 15 "the dogs" are used alongside those who practice magic arts, the sexually immoral, the murderers, the idolaters and everyone who loves and practices falsehood. These categories of people are also referred to as outsiders with regard to the eternal city. However, the word mutilator is not among this list. From this, we may say that Paul is borrowing the word "dogs" in order to refer to all evil workers and those who practice circumcision of the flesh, from the Jews who normally used it to refer to the Gentiles, (see Psalms 22: 16). This means that the three words are used to refer to the same group of people. Since he does not go on to say more about them, except that the Philippians and himself are said to be the true circumcision who do not glory in the flesh but in Christ Jesus, it means he is not referring to a specific or prominent circumcision party in the church in Philippi. Rather, he is warning them that such people would eventually be in their city. Perhaps, however, some of the believers in Philippi may have thought that circumcision and the Jewish way of life was the preferred way for Christians instead of Paul's Christian citizenship. In this way, Rome would not see Christians as a threat as they would simply be regarded as a branch of the recognized Jewish religion.[8] While this is possible, it is unlikely as any such Judaizing group does not appear to be prominent, given the friendly nature of this letter

---

[8]S. Fowl, p. 146f.

to all of the believers in Philippi, from beginning to end. However, these Judaizing Christians referred to as dogs were travelling from city to city, proudly showing themselves as the circumcised, since they enjoyed the protection of Rome and observed the Jewish rituals. From Acts, we know that those Jewish Christians, who believed that circumcision was necessary, were always a problem to Paul and his converts. As such, he was bound to warn the Philippians against them.[9] Moreover, even if they were not present in Philippi, they were still a potential threat to the Church in Philippi. Paul, therefore, warns the Christians in Philippi against them. Rather than go into detail about them, Paul prefers to spend more time explaining to the Philippians why circumcision and the law are unnecessary for Christians; hence Paul's personal example to begin this discussion, (see vv 4-11).

Paul, therefore, throws back the word "dogs" on Jews and the Jewish believers who were insisting that Gentiles must be circumcised to be fully Christian. He is thus borrowing the word that circumcised Jews and Judaizing Christians would have used of non-circumcised Christians. That the internal squabbles with regard to the Judaizing Christians are not so pronounced in Philippi is seen in the little time he gives to it.[10] Instead of telling us more about who they were, he goes on from vv. 4-14 to talk about himself, his experience whether in the past as a Jewish fanatic, o in Christ now and his hope for the future in his new life in Christ. He does this, as he does elsewhere, though differently, to prove to the Philippian Christians that they are "already children of the promises made to Abraham. They need do nothing more in terms of taking on the yoke of the Torah to situate themselves as heirs of Abraham." Since through faith in God, Abraham had that promise before he was circumcised, Gentiles, by faith in God's saving

---

[9]G. Fee, p. 294.
[10]S. Fowl, p.147; G. Fee, p.295; P. T. O'Brien, p. 364.

work in Christ, can also be "part of the Abrahamic covenant without being physically circumcised."[11] Paul, therefore, says that he and all who are with him and the Philippian Christians and other believers elsewhere who do not cling to circumcision of the flesh as a way of pleasing God or belonging to the covenant people of God, are the true circumcised ones and not those who are circumcised by physical mutilation of the flesh. It is the believers whose worship is directed by the Holy Spirit, the same believers who glory in Jesus Christ, and put no confidence in the flesh or in human ability, that are the true circumcision.

In v. 4, Paul goes on to tell them what he means by confidence in the flesh, using himself, what he was, what he has given up, where he is now and where he and the Philippians Christians who are the true circumcision, are going. First, is to have no confidence in the flesh. He has more reasons to put confidence in the flesh than they and anyone else, because he was circumcised on the eighth day, he is an Israelite, he is from the family of Benjamin, and he is a Hebrew to the core. Thus, by Paul's family tree, he is by blood a true Jew, unlike some of the advocates of Jewish Christianity who may have been proselytes or Gentile converts. He is not only a true Jew. He was a true and pious follower of the Jewish religion to the core, for with regard to the law, he was a Pharisee, and zealous in ensuring that the law was kept in its purest form, persecuting the church because he then thought they were perverting the law. Moreover, regarding righteousness based on the law, he says he was faultless. That is, he could not be found wanting in matters concerning the law. If the young and rich man who was looking for what to do to have eternal life could say he was keeping all the Ten Commandments, Saul, who is now Paul, could have done

---

[11]Fowl, pp. 147f; cf. Jeremiah 4: 4; 9: 25 - 26; Rom. 2: 25 - 29.

far more as a Pharisee.[12] We, therefore, need not doubt Paul regarding what he says of himself before becoming a Christian. This is more so when Paul is not known to be a flatterer or to give false testimony about himself.

Paul, therefore, is, saying here that if anyone thinks circumcision is the Christian way to live or to have salvation, he Paul has gone down that road as a legitimate, faithful and dedicated Jew in the Jewish faith and excelled in it. However, he has given up all these "advantages" because of his encounter with Jesus Christ on the road to Damascus. In him he now boasts or glories in and worships through the guidance of the Holy Spirit. Therefore, if anyone thinks there is anything to boast about circumcision, he had experienced or lived that life much better than anyone, but he has given it up because it is in no way comparable to life in Christ Jesus. Thus, by human standards or by the requirements of the Torah, Paul had considered himself a model Jew in every way. If others had grounds for confidence in the flesh, then he could match them at every point. In fact, he could surpass them, for he was a privileged member of the covenant people whom God had chosen for himself and set apart for holiness. Paul had responded in the appropriate way, even conforming to that righteousness rooted in the law. It called for infinite, painstaking effort, but he was able to make 'the grade, only to discover that it did him no good.[13]

---

[12]G. Fee, p. 309; O'Brien, p. 365; Fowl, p. 151; Bockmuehl, says, "The law which was a way of life was widely thought to be feasible and practical: for most faithful Jews it would have been absurd to think that God had given a revelation that could not in fact be lived out" (p. 202). And even in Christianity, Paul believes that the Philippians as Christians could be blameless and so he calls on them to behave in a way that they can "become blameless and pure children of God, faultless in the midst of crooked and perverted generation" (Phil. 2: 15).

[13]O'Brien, p. 381, citing F. F. Bruce, p. 85.

Paul, therefore, goes on to vv. 7-11 to show the Philippian Christians what being in Christ means to him now and for the future. Moreover, he shows how it surpasses what he experienced in Judaism, something that the Jewish Christians wanted to entice the Philippians into, even though what they have in Christ is far better. Paul is proud to say that he has given up all of this for the sake of Christ Jesus and the surpassing greatness of knowing him.

He expresses this in financial accounting terms in v. 7 saying, "But whatever was my gain, I consider these as loss because of Christ." What was thought in the flesh to be gain, profit or achievement is now in Christ a loss, deficit or shortfall. These fleshly achievements that he had thought to be gains or profit in the accounting books of heaven for him, he now, after encountering Christ, discovers to be loss, deficit or shortfall. What a surprising but heart-warming revelation! Indeed, he prefers all these to be loss or deficit to him because of "the surpassing value of knowing Christ Jesus, his Lord, "through whom everything is held together." Not only are they to be considered as loss. To truly gain Christ, he has to go to the extent of even considering such past achievements in Judaism as garbage, animal dung, or something awful.

Verse 9 states what it means to gain Christ. In Judaism, as he has already shown, it could be said that he had arrived religiously because he says that with regards to legalistic righteousness, he was faultless. However, having gained Christ, the righteousness he now possesses is not through his own effort in keeping the law, Rather, it is a righteousness that comes from God through faith in Christ Jesus. Such righteousness now compels Paul to want to know Christ Jesus the more. Moreover, he not only wants to know Jesus Christ the more, he also wants to know the power of his resurrection in this life. He wants to share in his suffering and in his death (v. 10) in this life, as Christ did. By so doing, Paul would attain to the resurrection of the dead at the return of Christ, which according to the next verse (v. 11), he is yet to attain, as against those who believe that the resurrection has already come and so they have the feeling of having already arrived or reached the state of perfection. Paul tells us plainly that some Christians in Corinth claimed to have attained this position (1 Cor. 4: 8 - 10).

Striving towards God's heavenly call, 3: 12 - 4: 1

[12]Not that I have already taken hold of it or I am already made perfect, but I also I strive to take hold of that for which I was seized by Christ Jesus. [13]Brothers, I myself do not claim I have obtained it. But one thing I do, forgetting the things that are behind and stretching ahead. [14]I strive toward the goal, to the prize of the heavenly call of God in Christ Jesus.

[15]Therefore, as far as we the mature have this mind and if anyone of you [the mature] should think otherwise, God will also reveal this to you.[16]Nevertheless, concerning what we have attained, [let us] walk in it.

[17]Brothers, be united in imitating me, and look out for those who walk as you have an example from us.[18]For many do walk as we have repeatedly told you, and also now say to you weeping, that they are enemies of the cross of Christ,[19] whose end is destruction, whose god is the stomach and whose glory is in their shame, setting their minds on earthly things. [20]For our citizenship is in heaven and from it we wait expectantly [for] a Saviour, the Lord Jesus Christ, [21] who will change our humble body and transform it into his glorious body.

Therefore, my beloved brothers and those whom I longed for, my joy and crown. Stand thus firm in the Lord, beloved.

By the time Paul reached v. 11, it dawned on him that the Philippians might be thinking that he felt he had arrived spiritually, which was what some Christians in Corinth thought. Therefore, in v. 12 Paul corrects any thought that he has already achieved what he had set out to accomplish in Christ. He makes it clear to the Philippian Christians that he has not already taken hold of or grasped the perfection he is talking of. Rather, he is yet to achieve perfection or be made perfect. His goal was still to continue to strive so as to take hold of that perfection for which Christ Jesus called him. Thus, he has not yet arrived or attained the state of perfection, as some false preachers were claiming. For him, he was still in the process of getting to take hold of it. He must still press on to take hold of the perfection which Christ had taken hold of him for. What that is, he does not say. All he is interested in telling the Philippian Christians and himself is that it is in sight, and that they must both press on to claim it.

Verse 13 does not tell us this thing that he is pressing on to claim. It simply repeats what is said in v. 12 for the purposes of emphasis and clarity. He does this by using the word "brothers," a word that portrays intimacy. He also does so by the use of athletic terms, saying, "Forgetting the things … behind" and "stretching ahead." "Brothers, I myself do not claim I have obtained it. But one thing I do, forgetting the things that are behind and stretching ahead," that is, to that which Christ seized him for. If he has not taken hold of it, what else is he to do to make sure he gets it? It is in v. 14 that gives us a clue of what that thing which he is straining himself or pressing on to take hold of. It is the prize for which God has called him heavenward in Christ Jesus. The key words right from vv. 12-14, are "to press on" or "to strive," "stretching ahead" and "forgetting," "overlooking" or "ignoring what is behind," with a view to taking hold or of grasping the prize that lies ahead. Some scholars like Fee and O'Brien, understand this prize to be

Christ, whom Paul will not know fully until the eschaton.[14] However, perhaps a better understanding of the prize is that it is the ultimate salvation for which Christ saved him. Thus it is a state of perfection.

Paul is unable to entirely forget his past because it is the memory of that surrendered past combined with the prospect of what is ahead that gives him the impetus to hold on to the new life for which Christ has chosen him. This makes him to press on or strive to have that prize. From time to time, he would reflect gratefully and humbly on his past. As Fowl notes, Paul has only conceived of his past from the perspective of one who is in Christ,

> . . . but it is not forgotten. In fact, it is only clear now, from the perspective of being in Christ, that Paul can offer a fruitful account of his past. His ability to 'press on toward the goal' can only be sustained by the truthful account of his past, which he is now able to [gratefully] narrate,"[15]

This is like a drunkard or a wayward person who has been saved by Christ, who now thinks of his past with tears and gratitude to God, as he reflects on what he is now and how he was about to destroy himself by his former way of life. The past is always for Paul a reminder to value what he now has, less it slips off and he is back to what is destructive.

Therefore, in vv. 12-14, Paul brings to mind what he had earlier said when talking about standing firm in the face of internal opposition because salvation still lies ahead of them (1: 28). They have not yet

---

[14]G. Fee, p. 346; O'Brien, who says, "In the immediate context the prize (*to brabeion*) is the full and complete gaining of Christ for whose sake everything else has been counted loss. The greatest reward is to know fully, and so to be in perfect fellowship with, the one who had apprehended Paul on the Damascus road. And this prize Paul wants his readers to grasp (p.433). O'Brien notes that W. Hendrickson says that the goal and prize point is Christ but that the goal is viewed " 'as the object of human striving' and fixes attention on the race that is being run", while the prize is " 'the gift of God's sovereign grace.'"

[15]Fowl, p. 161.

arrived. In 2: 12, he had asked them to work out their salvation with fear and trembling because God is at work in them. This is precisely what he is doing here, telling them he is still walking towards that salvation which he calls, "the prize of the upward call of God." They too must do the same, as he had said to them in 2: 12. Moreover, as in 2: 12, it is still God or Christ who is the motivating factor and actor in this. It is in him that Paul is able to press on steadfastly. In vv. 13f, he shows the way in which the race is run and that the winner is determined in the way in which the race is run (see I Corinthians 9: 27). For in both Philippians 3: 13f and I Corinthians 9: 27, the need for discipline is stressed.[16]

In verses 15 - 21 Paul applies what he has said about his own spiritual journey. In these verses, he wants the Philippians to emulate him and others instead of acting as the "dogs" are doing, consumed in their worldly achievements. He states this with an open mind, well aware that others may not share the same view with him. Thus, the classic statement in v. 15, which church leaders today need to hear loud and clear, "Therefore, as far as we the mature have this mind and if anyone of you [the mature] should think otherwise, God will also reveal this to you." Paul is talking here of the matured and not, as some scholars suppose, those who are perfect. (They assume this because they say he is using the same Greek word *(teleiein)* as in 3: 12). Neither is he being ironical as others supposed, because Paul would not classify himself as belonging to the *teleioi* (the perfect, the fully grown, the matured) whom he is critiquing here and elsewhere, (cf. 1 Cor. 4. 8 - 13). After all, he has already said in v. 12 that he has not yet arrived or reached perfection. Moreover, since we cannot say that he is being ironical in v. 12, neither can we say that he is being ironical in v. 15. We, therefore, have to think of another connotation for *teleios* that fits

---

[16]Fowl, p. 161.

what he is saying in this verse. The word *teleios* can be used to convey a variety of meanings including, perfect, complete, full grown, a morally developed person, mature, adult or manhood.[17]

Thus, as much as Paul expects all who are matured to share his view; as much as he thinks they should go the same way, he is not unaware of the fact that there may be some who do not, as in 1: 15. He did not mind this because Christ was being proclaimed in spite of the ill motives and the hurt it might have caused him. Paul is convinced God will also make things clear to those who think differently from him, since they belong to the matured (*teleioi*). Such people must be seen to live up to what is being pursued, which is, the prize of the upward call of God. In addition, they must be seen to be living out their common or communal life in accordance with the gospel and partnership with one another in the gospel.

Verse 16 therefore goes on to say, "Nevertheless, concerning what we have attained, let us walk in it," as a community and not individually, in spite of any differing perceptions, convinced that God will gradually reconcile them, as they walk together in what they have already attained. Thus, for Paul, the call to strive together with the same mind and spirit against external and internal problems, as we have seen so far right from 1: 27 to this point, is not a call to uniformity or sameness. It is rather a call to unity in diversity for the

---

[17]H. G. Liddell and R. Scott, *Greek-English Lexicon: With a Revised Supplement*; J. H. Mouton and G. Milligan, *The Vocabulary of the Greek Testament: Illustrated from the Papyri and other Non-Literary Sources*; Frederick W. Danker and Walter Bauer (Eds.), *A Greek-English Lexicon of the New Testament and Early Christian Literature*, 3rd Ed. sv. And O'Brien (p. 436) observes, Paul "employs *teleiein* elsewhere of those who are (actually or potentially) 'mature' in the Christian life: 1 Cor. 2: 6; 14: 20; Eph. 4: 13; Col. 1: 28; 4: 12). A similar rendering in this context that would be consistent with those other uses … We conclude then, that Paul is not writing ironically. Instead, he uses *teleioi* in a positive way to denote 'the spiritually mature.'"

common good, for there is beauty in diversity or variety. Unity in diversity shows the richness of God distributed to every individual in the believing community. O'Brien is, therefore, right in saying that by using the verb, *stoxein,* "to stand," the Philippians are being urged to move forward in unity. Recognizing that there may be differences of opinion, the apostle desires that the whole community should move forward together. He is not encouraging the presence of 'spiritual virtuosos,' to use F. W. Beare's expression; as Christians they need to be united in the contest in which all are engaged, working towards the same goal and ready to help one another, especially in bearing one another's burdens, "the actual practice of which he takes in v. 17."[18]

Christians today have not learned to live within this rich diversity in God's creation and to appreciate it, even though we talk so much about unity. This was one of the problems of the Corinthian church and it is still the one of the problems of the church today. We do not know how to live with varieties of gifts and enjoy them in every member of the church. Leaders are divided and members are divided over big and minor issues and particularly over mundane things like positions and material things that may not last longer than our lifetime, let alone to eternity. The church cannot expect to carry the day in this era of globalisation, terrorism and anti-Christian forces unless it takes on board this common "standard of thinking, feeling and acting," to use Fowl's expression. Even more than that, Christians cannot expect to "take hold of the prize" promised us unless we listen to Paul and "walk in line with what we have attained" in the gospel as a believing people

---

[18]O'Brien, p. 441f; BAGD, p. 769; G. Delling pp. 666-669; F. W. Beare, p. 132; Fowl, pp. 165f who says that the "military image of keeping in line or in step" which this word conveys. It "speaks of a common pattern of behaviour, conformed to a particular standard." Thus, Paul is calling on the Philippians to copy him, to fall into line with the example that he sets.

and not individually. We need to think, feel and act in a common fashion as one people with our heavenly destiny in mind, where this common good way of thinking, feeling and acting will be fully realized and practiced.[19]

It is in this context that we see Paul in v. 17 referring to the Philippians again as brothers (sisters included) and calling on them to be united in imitating him as well as to "look out for those who walk as you have an example from us." He does not see himself as the only one who is already walking the way he has been calling them to walk or live. There is no arrogance in his call to imitate him, especially as he also refers to others who are worthy of emulation.[20] Moreover, he is also going to mention Christians who were bad examples to the Philippian Christians, who may find their way into their church, if they are not already there.

Further, he also reiterates his call that all of them who belong to the citizenship of the gospel (1: 27) should be united in living out their lives in accordance with what the community has attained so far. Here again, we see the same emphasis on working together as a united community of believers. In a community where individualistic living thrives, no one either dares to call others to emulate him or her nor does anyone emulate anyone else. This is what accounts for the decline of Christianity in our postmodern society. The fear of being mocked, with people accusing us of being arrogant, self-righteous or having a "holier-than-thou" attitude deters people. Nor do Christians

---

[19]Fowl, p. 166.

[20]The fact that "we" could refer to "I" among Greek writers of the time, which also agrees with the singular "example" (tupos), does not necessarily mean Paul is still referring to himself here and not to other Christians with him and those in Philippi who should be emulated. This is because such would be in with the immediate context and the context of the letter to the Philippians as a whole. See O'Brien, p. 449f who also cites W. P. De Boer, Imitation, p. 183.

want to be examples worthy of emulation. Yet whether or not others emulate us is not something we have much choice about; we are always influencing others either positively or negatively. We are all being emulated, positively or negatively, whether we like it or not. Therefore, if we must live out our lives according to the gospel as Christians, we must look out for these two groups of people, one to emulate and the other to avoid emulating.

Those who are mature and know their purpose in life know that some people need to be discipled and others are tasked with the responsibility to disciple others. Those discipling other people should always strive to be good examples to their disciples. Moreover, they cannot be ashamed or shy away from telling their disciple(s) to imitate them. Calling disciples to become like their mentors is imperative when there are many teachers with aspirations and desires that are contrary to the gospel, (cf. vv. 18-19).

In vv. 18-19, Paul does not hesitate to warn the Christians in Philippi concerning those Christians they are likely going to come across whom they should avoid, if they are to live their lives according to his instructions. He does not mention such Christians with any sense of pride and arrogance but with sorrow and tears in his eyes. Paul feels that such Christians or preachers are not aware they are slipping away from the truth they knew and walked in previously. These Christians, Paul describes in these verses are people, "who are enemies of the cross of Christ," whose "god is their stomach," "who glory in their shame" and people whose "mind is on earthly things" and not on the things of God. Again, as in 3: 2, Paul does not go any further to tell us who they are, nor whether they are already in Philippi or if he is just anticipating that they will definitely come to Philippi. He does not say they are false teachers but that their walk or life is contrary to the way Paul has been advocating.[21] Nor does he say whether they are definitely Christians. However, the way he describes them gives the impression that they are. Paul is not so concerned about this, as scholars are today, but he is very concerned to render their position void and, in the strongest of terms, to warn his readers against their way of life. As to who these enemies of the cross are, Fowl rightly observes:

> Whoever these believers are, we assume that as Christians they did not set out to become enemies of the cross, neither would they have characterized themselves that way..... Instead, we should understand that these Christians were seeking to live faithful lives. Through various practices, lack of proper attention to the ways in which seemingly good decisions misdirected their lives, through a failure to have their thoughts, feelings, and actions appropriately directed by Christ, they slowly and imperceptibly became enemies of the cross. It is only when we see these people in this light that we can begin to imagine how easily friends of the cross can be transformed into enemies of the cross and to see how Paul's admonitions here could apply to us.[22]

This explains why Paul weeps for such Christians. It is painful and sad to see a Christian who knows the benefits that there are in being a Christian, but instead of standing firm, gradually drifts away through lack of watchfulness to live out his or her Christian life in accordance with the gospel and who fails to hear the collective voice calling him or her to beware.

As in v. 3, v. 20 states who the Philippians and Paul are, as against what these other people are. The other Christians are worldly bound but Paul and the Philippians are heavenly bound, saying, "For our

---

[21]G. Fee, pp. 367f.
[22]Fowl, p. 172.

citizenship is in heaven and from it we wait expectantly [for] a Saviour, the Lord Jesus Christ." This takes us back to 1: 27 again, where he had told the Philippians to live their citizenship life only according to the gospel. These other Christians are described as enemies of the cross, while Paul and the Philippians are citizens of heaven and live here and now as citizens of heaven. As citizens of heaven, they expectantly wait for a Saviour from heaven, the Lord Jesus Christ. When he comes, he will change their lowly body into his glorious body. Thereafter, he will usher them into the anticipated heavenly citizenship, which he has been trying to ask them to strive to take hold of.

Chapter 4: 1, therefore, stands as a fitting conclusion to 3: 21, since Christ has not yet come to change their lowly bodies into his glorious body. As they wait for this, he reminds them of the necessity of standing firm. As he instructed regarding facing external opponents, so he instructs in the case of internal enemies of the cross. Nevertheless, since he is not done with the internal problems, he is bringing the exhortation to stand firm here probably because the internal problems are in two categories. The first part, which he has already dealt with, has to do with people opposed to the way of life of the church. The problem now remaining, concerns two leaders of the church who, along with others have faithfully laboured with Paul in the gospel, but are now in disagreement with each other.

The verse first expresses Paul's closeness to the Philippians, calling them, "my beloved brothers whom I also greatly longed for" and "my joy and crown." Paul, right from the beginning of the letter has not hidden his closeness with the Philippians by his use of intimate words like, "brothers' (sisters inclusive). He has used brother in 1: 12; 3: 1, 13, 17 and will do so in 4: 8. He uses similar intimate expressions of the church in Thessalonica in 1 Thessalonians 2: 19 (our hope, joy and crown). Paul's expression of deep love for the Philippian church runs through the letter, as found in 1: 7 "have you in my heart", 1: 8, "I long for all of you with the affection of Christ" and 2: 12, "my dear friends" and then here in 4: 1, "my beloved brothers whom I also greatly longed for" and "my joy and crown." He has also already shown they are his joy in 1; 4; 2: 2 and here in 4: 1 and 10, "my joy and crown. As O'Brien rightly notes, they are his joy and crown not only at the return of Christ, but even now they are his delight and reward or trophy in the preaching of the gospel.[23] Thus, Paul openly shows how dear the Philippian church is to him, by his use of very intimate terms of friendship with them. Fowl is, therefore, right in saying that this dispels any idea that there is a serious problem in the church in Philippi or that there is problem between them and Paul, as we find in Corinth. This intimacy calls for accountability between them. Thus, the intimacy makes him to be frank and plain both to the church and to Euodia and Syntyche, who are in disagreement. He acknowledges the two women leaders have laboured with him in the gospel.

The church today ought to emulate this kind of intimacy and accountability without discrimination or without taking sides. For, lack of indiscriminate intimacy and accountability is the cause of disagreements and divisions in the church of God, making the church vulnerable to attack from within and without.

The importance of joy in church's life, makes Paul mention it here so as to help him transition smoothly from what he has been saying to what he is about to raise. Again he goes back to the same charge in 1: 27 of standing firm in one spirit, struggling together with one mind, and remaining steadfast in the gospel. Now they are to practice these qualities in the midst of their internal problems, whereas previously (in 1: 27 – 30) Paul had been referring to external opponents.[24] Here,

---

[23] O'Brien, pp. 475f.
[24] Fowl p. 176ff.

very briefly, he says, "Stand firm in the Lord." They are not to be shaken by those Christians who have become worldly or have become enemies of the cross nor are they to be shaken by the disagreements between the two leaders of the church, Euodia and Syntyche. Rather they should stand firm and see that the two are reconciled. As has been said repeatedly, they are not to stand firm individually but as a community so that these opponents or problems may not intimidate them. In addition, as he had said earlier, they are to stand firm by steadfastly fighting together with one mind and spirit. This should be done with their salvation in sight, knowing very well that God is at work in them doing this (1: 27f; 2: 12 - 13). They accomplish this by living in harmony with one another and they are to strive together steadfastly until they make it to the time of the Lord's return, when their lowly bodies will be changed to the Lord's glorious body, to God's own praise and honour.

Living in harmony, 4: 2 - 3

> [2]I plead with Euodia and I plead with Syntyche to agree with one another in the Lord. [3]Yes, and I ask you true fellow workers, assist them, they are …. in the gospel with me and with Clement and the rest of my fellow workers whose names are in the book of life.

Verse 2, first of all, pleads with the two leaders, Euodia and Syntyche, "I plead with Euodia and I plead with Syntyche to agree with one another in the Lord." By the use of the Greek word *parakalein (to plea*, *to beg)*, Paul is not commanding these two women whom he describes as colleagues, to agree. Although the word can be used in the sense of "summon" or "urge," it is to be understood here and in most places where Paul uses the word, in the sense of "to plead with," "to beg" or "to beseech."[25] Besides that, the manner in which he addresses them also suggests that Paul is confident that the problem between the two women can be overcome. Paul's positive evaluation of the two shows that they are church leaders and not the names of two groups of people in the church, as some argue. The way he addresses them by name also shows the seriousness of the disagreement between them and its implications for the church's unity. Even though he was aware the letter was to be read in public, to the hearing of every member, he still addresses them by name in a forceful way, "I plead with Euodia and I plead with Syntyche," repeating the word "I plead" before each of the name. This also shows that Paul is not taking sides,[26] but he remains neutral, the mark of a leader known for his integrity.

Paul pleads with them to think the same way in the Lord and not in their own individual perception and personal interest. Solutions to disagreements can usually only be reached when those disagreeing make compromises. Paul does not tell us what the dispute was all about. Feminist theologians like Marchal, and Fiorenza argue that that the two women were in disagreement with Paul's theological stance, which favoured Roman imperial policy. If we are to do any reconstruction from what Paul is saying here, we can only say that the two are in disagreement over either of two issues or both:

1. that one of them is in agreement with Paul and the other is not or
2. the two are in disagreement over some issues between them perhaps personal, theological or administrative in nature.

The second is the most likely because of the praises Paul heaped on the two women. If they were in disagreement with him, he would

---

[25]See O'Brien, p. 477 who cites C. J. Bjerkelund, Parakalo, pp. 174-176 and W. Schenk, p. 271 in 2 of the two usages.
[26]O'Brien, p. 478.

have put them in the same category with the internal enemies of the cross of 3: 18f. Moreover, there is nothing in these verses or in the letter to show that Paul was pro-Rome and these women leaders, who happened to be Greeks, were not in support of Paul's position. They were two women with whom Paul had worked closely in spreading the gospel, and he had confidence in both of them. Hence, he wanted other church leaders to help them overcome their disagreement and restore unity. The church had to maintain its unity if it was to overcome both its internal and external opponents. They should sit down together, iron out their differences, and come to an agreement on how to work in harmony with each other. As they do so, they are to do it in the way the Lord would like them and not on their own individual terms. The idea that they should sit together and iron out the disagreement between them fits in with the general idea of the letter; that is that the church should steadfastly fight together any force militating against it (1: 27 - 30). Paul had also talked of humility and self-sacrifice after the life of Christ, instead of each seeking after his or her interest (2: 1 - 11). Paul's teaching is also in harmony with Jesus' directive that believers should reconcile where one has offended another or one feels he or she has been offended (Matthew 5: 21 - 27; 18: 15 - 17).

To allow harmony to reign between one another and within the believing community is a way of walking or lifestyle that is worthy of the gospel and of the heavenly citizenship they have been called into. As citizens of heaven, we are called to a peaceful and harmonious co-existence in the believing community we are members of. If there will be no division in heaven between believers, there should be a foretaste of this in the first place here on earth as we are already citizens of heaven here and now. The two prominent women in the church therefore are exhorted to live in harmony with one another, because not only is it tearing the two personalities apart but also because this is unbecoming of citizens of heaven and it is a threat to the unity of the church.

Because of its seriousness, Paul in v. 3a asks one of his fellow workers to help them do this and not to leave them to do it by themselves as if it were their thing and their thing alone: "Yes, and I ask you my true fellow worker, assist them." He is to act on behalf of the church to save the church from being affected by this dispute. Scholars debate who this person is. However, there is no need to speculate. This fellow-worker was obviously well known in Philippi and judged capable of carrying out this responsibility.[27] Just as Paul addressed the believers in Corinth who were sitting on the fence when a young man committed the sin of incest (I Corinthians 5: 1 - 11), in the same way, he does not want the believers in Philippi to sit on the fence while these two women tear each other and the church apart. If we are partners in Christ, then what happens to one person, or between two people, or among a group of people happens to the entire believing community. Hence, it is always right to resolve rifts between people in the church. True partnership in the gospel is living in harmony with one another and not harming one another in any way or allowing differences to tear the church or individual members apart.

In v. 3b, Paul sets out his reasons for reconciling the two women, apart from the fact that division is not good for the church. These women, Clement and the rest of his fellow-workers contended or struggled together with him in the preaching of the gospel and their names are written in the book of life. In spite of the problem between them, Paul has not forgotten their past fruitful labour. He has not written them off because they have a disagreement between them. Nor is he taking sides. Even though he is not prepared to close his eyes to the seriousness of the disagreement, he is also not prepared to

---

[27] See O'Brien, p. 480 for these names.

close his eyes to their past good work in the church. Indeed, their past good work is the motivation for reconciliation. Problems are bound to come between Christians, and problems are bound to be resolved between Christians, if the church is to walk according to the gospel. If the church is the church of God, there are always gifted and faithful believers in the church who are capable of resolving such problems. To show that we are walking according to the gospel is to face problems squarely without burying them in the sand. As Paul himself says to the Corinthians in 1 Corinthians 5: 1 - 11, there are always people or someone in the church, as in the Church in Philippi, who are capable of doing this. There are bound to be some leaders in the church who are gifted in conflict resolution. That is why it is good to know who is who in a church and their spiritual gifts, talents and professions, all of which are necessary for building the church in a holistic way. Paul insists that they must be assisted in the effort to resolve the disagreement because they have laboured with him in the gospel.

It is very common today to rubbish the past good work of men and women of God when they fall short. While we should not bury problems or the failings of members and leaders of the church in the sand, because of its effects on the church and the individual, in similar manner we cannot rubbish their good works simply because they fail in one area. A balance must be kept between the two and that balance is to carefully and sensitively assist the parties concerned to think together and to think sacrificially and in the interest of one another and the church. They should come to an agreement in a way that the interests of the two and of the church are taken into account.

Next, Paul says that they should be given a helping hand to come to that agreement because their names are written in the book of life along with others who have laboured with Paul and with other believers. In disagreements between people, it is common for one or both parties to rubbish the other as firewood for hell or as the devil incarnate. However, this is not the case with Paul. When we believe, and our names are written in the book of life, it is not that easy for one's name to be erased. God does not write anyone off when he falls but raises him or her from the ground or the pit and washes them. This may or may not be not painful, depending on who God is dealing with. However, he does not rubbish him or her, unless the person persists to go his or her own way. The work of the church or Christians therefore is to build and not tear down and we the individuals constitute the church. Hence, Paul insists that the Philippians should walk together as a church, not as individuals, together facing their opponents who wage war against the church. In Galatians 6: 1f, he says, "Brothers, if someone is caught in a sin, you who are spiritual should restore him gently. But watch (out) yourself, or else you also may be tempted. Carry each other's burdens, and in this way you will fulfil the law of Christ."

Be joyful, patient and content, 4: 4 - 9

[4]Rejoice in the Lord always. Again, I say rejoice. 5Let all men know your forbearance, the Lord is near. [6]Do not be anxious in any way, but in everything by prayer and petition with thanksgiving let your request be made known to God. [7]And the peace of God which surpasses all reasoning, will guard your heart and your thoughts in Christ Jesus.

[8]Finally, brothers, whatever is true, whatever is honourable, whatever is righteous, whatever is holy, whatever is lovely, whatever is worthy of praise, if there is any moral excellence, if there is any praiseworthy thing, reflect on these things. [9]And what you learned, received, heard and saw in me, live and practice them. And the God of peace will be with you.

As Paul comes close to the end of exhorting them over the internal problems that threatened the unity and survival of the church, he calls them to a life of rejoicing, despite the problems. He did just the same in 3: 1, after discussing the external opposition against the church, however now in much more detail than previously. Many of the rifts that arise between members or between leaders in the church are due to their failure to rejoice in the Lord. That is, failure to rejoice over what God has done for each of us in Christ Jesus, and over God's many blessings in spite of our failings in his service. Leaders often forget that the positions they occupy in God's church, and even in society, are acts of grace and not our merits before God. And their leadership is also based on the good will of the people and not so much what we have done for those who elect us into positions of leadership. Because we fail to realize this, we often fail to rejoice in his grace and the good will of the people. Instead of rejoicing, we become insecure about the positions we occupy. Or we become jealous about the positions others occupy either above or beneath us, thinking those beneath us are plotting to unseat us or envying those above us. Worse still, we go hunting for those who did not elect us or are not in support of our views. All of these take us miles away from rejoicing in the goodness of the Lord in our lives, and in the lives of the rest of God's people. As a result, we become impatient with one another, fail to bear with one another's failings, and as a result, rifts slip in between leaders and members, thus, dividing the church of God.

Knowing the importance of rejoicing even in the midst of problems, Paul calls on the entire church to always rejoice in the Lord, and be patient with one another rather than to indulge in disagreements, such as between Euodia and Syntyche. Instead, they are to have the same mind and spirit, as they steadfastly pursue the salvation that lies ahead and fight together against any external enemy that would hinder them from taking hold of it. For Paul, they should be seen to be forbearing, self-controlled, and patient towards one another.

In addition, for Paul, one other reason for rejoicing and patience is that the Lord's return is near. In view of the Lord's near return, Paul says that anxiety about leadership positions, about wellbeing, about what we do or about anything at all, becomes irrelevant. Instead, they should be devoting themselves as a community to prayer, petitions and thanksgiving to God. The result of this would be "the peace of God which surpasses all reasoning," would be their portion. That is, this peace of God, which surpasses our reasoning abilities that sometimes divide us or tear us apart, will guard their minds, hearts and thoughts against any divisive attitudes as they worship and serve the Lord together and as they interact with one another as a believing community.

Chapter 4: 4 - 9, therefore ends this section (3: 1 - 4: 9) with a call to rejoice in the Lord always and not to worry. Apart from rejoicing over their position in Christ, they are to let their gentleness or forbearance be prominent to everyone as well as make known their request to God in prayer, no matter what problems there may be. Rather than live in disagreement, they should always rejoice in the Lord and allow gentleness and lack of anxiety be evident to all within and without the church (vv. 4-6a). As a community, they should focus their attention on whatever is true, honourable, righteous, holy, lovely, worthy of praise and of moral excellence. Whatever they have learned, received, heard and seen in Paul, they should reflect on and live or practice them. It is by so doing that they would have their peace (vv. 7-9).

In v. 4, twice he calls the Philippians to rejoice in the Lord as he previously did in 3: 1, in spite of the opposition they faced. True Christianity is not a religion that robs one of joy, but it is full of joy no matter the circumstances. True Christianity calls believers into a life of rejoicing in the God we believe in, because of the countless privileges we have through his saving work in Christ Jesus. The joy of the Christian is not dependent on his circumstances or on what he is able to do or achieve, but it is in the Lord. Our joy is derived from what God has done for us in Christ Jesus. As O'Brien says, the Philippians are to keep on rejoicing in the Lord regardless of their circumstances.[28] This reminds us of what Paul and Silas experienced at the beginning of their ministry in Philippi, when they were arrested and imprisoned. As they sat in prison in chains, they began to sing songs of praise to God that night (Acts 16:15) instead of mourning over their unjust treatment. Paul had already told them of his attitude towards his imprisonment in 1: 12 - 26. Rejoicing in the Lord for Paul, therefore, is critical in the Christian walk with God. Peace from God is the confirmation of our being in Christ. That is why we can rejoice despite of the circumstances we find ourselves in.

Since he does not go on to elaborate on their need to rejoice, we may not see the call to rejoice as simply referring to the joy at the return of Christ. He is calling on them to learn to rejoice in their present circumstances as well as to rejoice in the eternal life to come. The fact that the eternal life they have, begins here and now, means that they are already having a foretaste of what is to come in its full manifestation at the return of Christ. This calls, therefore, for rejoicing whatever be the condition they find themselves in now, since what awaits them outweighs the suffering they may be currently going through.

At first thought, it is hard to see the connection between this and v. 5, where he asks that their gentleness should be made evident to all people, referring not only to their fellow believers, but also to unbelievers. However, this is a theme of Paul's that can be traced through the book as he speaks of gentleness, self-sacrifice, self-control, and humility in the midst of opposition. The verse is concluded with the statement, "The Lord is near" which doesn't seem to be related to

---

[28]O'Brien, p. 485.

gentleness. However, it does explain v. 4 that sets out the context for the command to be gentle. Because the Lord is near they should not only be gentle in character and with other believers, but also be known more widely for their gentleness. They need to act responsibly and should not be known for taking the law into their own hands because the Lord, who is with them, will act in his time and on their behalf (cf. James 5: 7 - 8). Some scholars suggest that, "the Lord is near" (Greek: *eggus*) refers only to the *eschaton* and not that he is present in their midst. However, Paul had already said in 2: 13 that God is at work in them for his pleasure as they work out their salvation with fear and trembling (2: 12). Both aspects of the statement are, therefore, important. It is in this context that the next imperative in v. 6 should also be understood. Because the Lord God is near or is with them and the return of the Lord Jesus is not far away, they are not to worry over the opposition and problems confronting them, or to allow these issues to overwhelm and divide them. Instead, despite the struggles they are experiencing, they should be steadfast, united and be gentle towards everyone. Moreover, they are to make known their requests and petitions to God who is near and working powerfully in them in their circumstances. To worry shows a lack of trust in God's care and power to save. Instead, they should be thankful knowing that they are more than conquerors through Christ who loves them and strengthens them (Rom. 8: 37). The result of this says, v. 7, is that "the peace of God which surpasses all reasoning will guard their hearts and thoughts" in Christ Jesus.

Verses 8-9 serve as a conclusion to both the external and internal problems discussed in the letter so far and not as an ending to the letter as supposed by some. These verses also say what it means to stand firm in the Lord. So that by *loipos, aᵗelphos* in v. 8, Paul would again be saying, "The bottom line, brethren," is that whatever is true, honourable, righteous, holy, lovely, worthy of praise and of moral excellence, they should reflect on these. This applies to what has been said so far and all other things that are worthy of reflecting on. It also includes what they have learned, and seen in Paul. As they make their requests and petitions known to the Lord and fix their minds on whatever is right and true, the joy and peace of the Lord will guard their hearts and thoughts over whatever is right. All the more so when the believing community encourages each other to remain steadfast in Christ.

Paul is not restricting these virtues to what is spiritually true, since these virtues or values are also found among the Stoic and Cynic moral philosophers. The "whatever" covers anything that is true and honourable or worthy of praise, wherever it is found. The earth is the Lord's and all that is therein. Believers should carefully reflect in their minds whatever is true so that they may be able to shape their behaviour in a way that is in line with the gospel.[29] This also means that they are not to take in anything that appears to be right or noble at first sight or at first hearing, for it is not everything that appears to be worthy of praise. As he says in 1 Corinthians 6: 12ff, it is not everything that is lawful that is worth doing, because it is not everything that is beneficial. This is worth noting in our day when the church accepts anything that the unbelieving world does. The church should not be doing things simply because everybody does it or because it is the fashion or convention of the day. It is only when the church is conscious of this and guards against this, by walking according to the gospel, instead of walking the way of the unbelieving world that the peace of God will be with his church, even in the midst of external oppositions or internal problems militating against it.

---

[29]See G. F. Hawthorne, p. 185; O'Brien, p. 502f.

Questions for further reflection and study

1.   Did these mutilators or earthly bound Christians know they were enemies of Christ? What can we learn from their position?
2.   Discuss the personal testimony of Paul and his giving up of his fleshly achievements to follow Jesus and pursue what he had called him for.
3.   Discuss Paul's attitude towards the disagreement of Euodia and Syntyche.
4.   How can we be joyful in the midst of persecution or suffering?

PAUL REJOICES OVER THEIR GIFT AND MORE OVER ITS BENEFITS TO THEM, 4: 10 - 20

[10]But I greatly rejoice in the Lord that you have now resumed the concern you had for me, a concern that you set your minds on, but you had no opportunity. [11]I say this not because I lack, for I have learned to be content in whatever circumstances I am in. [12]I know also how to live with little and I know how to live in flourishing state. In any and every situation, I have learned to have plenty to eat and to be hungry, to flourish and to be in want. [13]I have all the strength by the power that is in me [in Christ to do so]. [14]Nevertheless, you have done well, having shared with me in my suffering.

[15]But you should also know this, Philippians, that in the beginning of the gospel, when I came from Macedonia, no church shared with me in the giving and receiving the word, except you alone.[16]And that in Thessalonica you also more than once sent support for my livelihood. [17]Not that I desire the gift [you sent], but I desire the fruit which increases in your account. [18]And I have received full payment and abundantly so. I have been fully supplied having received from Epaphroditus that which is from you, a fragrant offering, an acceptable

sacrifice, very pleasing to God. [19]And my God will fill every
need of yours according to his riches in glory in Christ Jesus.
[20]And to my God and Father be glory forever and ever. Amen.

Giving thanks during Paul's time was also a worthwhile thing to do.
However, giving thanks had its implications as well. A look at what
giving thanks meant in the Greco-Roman context of Paul's time will
help us appreciate the manner in which Paul gave thanks, and the time
he devoted to giving thanks for what he received from the church.

To the African, giving thanks for what is given to one is the right
thing to do and this can be done in either words and/or cash or kind.
To fail to give thanks in many African cultures for some good done
to one by another is regarded as a mark of ingratitude. However, in
some contexts, to give thanks repeatedly is seen as a sign of asking
for more. Apart from that, to give thanks in most cases is a mark of
contentment and the cementing of the relationship with the giver.
However, giving thanks can be associated with feelings of superiority
and inferiority, so much so that one may, when first offered the gift,
refuse something, even when one wants it or is in need, eventually
relenting after persuasion. In such a case, some may not even give
thanks for the good done to them because they feel it will make the
giver feel superior over them. However, not so for Paul. This is evident
in this letter and in his other letters. In Paul's understanding, to give
thanks for what has been given, is a mark of recognition and a desire to
partner with the persons who have shared from their riches and in his
wants or needs. This is similar to what we find in the Greco-Roman
era of Paul's time.

Regarding placing the thanksgiving here, some scholars have
wondered why Paul leaves the very important issue, which the letter
opens with, until now. Others see its placement here as simply a
preliminary for the closing matter. In other words, some feel that Paul

must have a purpose for leaving his thanksgiving for the gift sent to him by the Philippians to the end of the body of the letter while others say this is simply a part of his closing remarks and is not a major section in the body of the letter. However, since thanksgiving for the gift was introduced in the opening of the letter, this one has to be seen as a major section of the body of the letter. Paul had to treat this important subject matter somewhere in the body of the letter and he felt it is better placed toward the end, because this subject is a fitting closure of the issue of working together to further the gospel that the body has been taking about. As such, it is better seen as part of the body of the letter than a part of the closing remark.

Some scholars also wonder why Paul does not show clearly that he is giving thanks for what the Philippians have sent to him to solve his needs. Instead of making it very clear that he is giving thanks, he rather stresses that what interests him most about the gift is that it has increased or swelled up their bank accounts in heaven. He is also very clear in telling them that he has learned how to flourish or prosper, both in times of want as well as in times of plenty. Thus, a close look at these verses, shows:

a. Paul moving between giving thanks and explaining away that thanks by saying that he has learned how to be content or

b. Paul is saying that they have done a good job in sending the gift and describing the gift in lofty words and yet he turns to say that what counts most to him in the gift is the benefits that accrue to the Philippian's heavenly bank account.

All these, plus leaving this important issue to the end of the body of the letter have bothered scholars about Paul's thanksgiving in this letter. While Greco-Roman social and rhetorical conventions on giving and receiving between friends will be helpful in understanding Paul, a careful look at the verses will help reduce undue reconstruction. Any worthwhile reconstruction must be based on a close examination of the text and the Greco-Roman texts on giving and receiving can only be examined to see if they fit in with what Paul is saying in Philippians, rather than the other way round.

Therefore, while Paul expresses his appreciation to the Philippians for their gift to him, he does so from the angle of contentment, lest his thanksgiving be seen as asking for more. The gift expressed the importance of partnership in the gospel and in material possessions. Paul's appreciation and acceptance of their gift is an important aspect of that partnership, crucial in cementing their bond. Partnership entails giving and receiving, not only giving or only receiving. However, Paul goes further than simply giving thanks for their gift, but he goes on to tell them what giving is and what it does for the giver and receiver. This helps us not to make the mistake of seeing Paul as simply trying to avoid giving thanks because of the implications about giving and receiving in his day. Knowing that, will help us to look carefully at what he wants to achieve in these verses.

Paul first mentions his thanks for their gift in 1:3–11, and modern readers would normally expect him to have dealt with it fully then, not leaving the full explanation until 4:10–20. However, Paul wants to deal with what really constitutes partnership in the gospel first. While partnership in material possessions is part of partnership in the gospel, it goes beyond that. He also needs to talk about what true partnership in the gospel entails, plus the barriers that stand in the way of that partnership. Chapter 4: 10 - 20 is, therefore, far more than simply a thanksgiving for what the Philippian church sent to him. It is a mixture of thanksgiving, talk on material contentment, and seeking the benefits of others rather than one's own benefit. In other words, while for Paul, this giving is a good thing, a fragrant offering to God worth giving thanks for, it also had great implications for the nature of their continued relationship with Paul and the proclamation of the gospel. Knowing the implications of giving in Greco-Roman world, and even today in Africa, Paul's response to their gift was not going to be simply a straight thank you, but thank you with a lesson or teaching on material contentment and seeking the benefits of others. Being that is the case, it is only right that Paul leaves this toward the end of the letter, as a closure to the body of the letter before the actual closing remarks.

When the modern reader sees it from this perspective, the contradictions and lack of coherence that are often seen by some scholars disappear. In 1: 12 - 2: 30, Paul makes it clear that he and the Philippians are facing the same suffering for the same reasons and in the hands of the same external opponents (1: 30). His own suffering has turned out to be for the good of the gospel, because the palace guards have come to know that he is in prison for his faith and not for any crime committed. Further, many preachers have, because of his imprisonment, taken up preaching the gospel without fear. Even though some have taken up the preaching of the gospel for the wrong reason, for injuring his person, this does not matter for Paul, since Christ is being preached. For this reason, the Philippians too must be steadfast and must fight together against their opponents. They should do that, not with carnal weapons, but with spiritual weapons. Moreover, they should do this, not individually but corporately, with one mind and spirit and with their salvation in sight (1: 28). In 3: 1 - 4: 9, he draws their attention to the fact that there are as well internal opponents and they need to respond positively to strife in their midst. All this should be done with joy and thanksgiving and not grumbling.

Having done that, he is now in a position to express his joy over their resumption of concern for him, a concern that they had at the beginning, but for one reason or the other, they had stopped showing. In 1: 3 - 11, he had given thanks for their partnership in the gospel from the beginning until the time of writing the letter. Having dealt with the issues that are more of a threat to their partnership, Paul can now turn to an issue of rejoicing over their gift and what it meant to him and what it has yielded for the Philippians who sent it.

Reasons for resumption of support, v. 10

Verse 10 therefore opens up the last subject matter of the letter by the transition formula, "I rejoice greatly in the Lord." Only in Colossians 1: 24, do we have this same formula used; "Now I rejoice in what was suffered for you." The interesting feature is that he is rejoicing in the Lord over their action and not giving thanks directly to them for the gift. Whereas in 1: 3, he gives thanks, although not really to them but to God, in prayer for their partnership in the gospel with him, here in v. 10, he says he rejoices in the Lord that they have resumed their concern for him. This is an action that they had set their minds to do, but had not yet had the opportunity to do so. As Fowl and other scholars rightly observe, to give thanks had a lot of implications during Paul's time. Fowl puts it, "A straightforward expression of thanks would invoke the very social conventions about status and reciprocity that Paul seeks here to circumscribe, if not undermine."[1] Thus, his contemporaries the Stoics and Cynics, and even some of his readers would have seen exuberant joy over the gift in a bad light.

Therefore, instead of expressing his joy over the gift, thus attracting criticism, he expresses his joy over the resumption of the partnership, which of course is symbolised by the gift. He acknowledges that the break in their mutual link hadn't been anyone's fault, but simply due to a lack of opportunity on the Philippians' part. However, he rejoices

---

[1]Fowl p. 192; Bockmuehl, pp. 260f.

that the link has been restored, especially for what it does for the Philippians.

This explains why the joy over the gift is not mentioned in vv. 11-13, but is spoken of here in vv. 14-16 and 18. Thus, as Fowl puts it:

> No doubt, Paul is grateful to the Philippians. Nevertheless, by phrasing the issue this way at the outset, Paul makes it clear that he and the Philippians are not in a conventional relationship of reciprocity. Because issues of giving and receiving are also bound up in issues of power and status, it is crucial for Paul to make it clear to the Philippians that they and he are common partners in God's work; their care for each other always has this element in view.[2]

Reason for rejoicing, vv. 11 - 13

In vv. 11-13 therefore, Paul quickly explains why he is rejoicing, less it be misunderstood that he is asking for more. He is not appreciating them for the resumption of their support so that they would continue to financially support to him from now on, as they used to do. Paul isn't denying the fact that he is in need, because he had earlier in 2: 25 said that he had needs and that they had sent Epaphroditus to meet those needs. Fowl cites Petermann who referred to Seneca's, *De Beneficiis* 2.2.2; 7.24.2, which says that a mere mention of "one's lack of something, could imply a request for that thing."[3] As Bockmuehl puts it, "Paul does not deny his lack of resources; indeed in 2: 25 he was not embarrassed to admit to his readers that Epaphroditus had been "your minister to my need (*chreia*)"[4] Yet, although he is in need, he is not implicitly asking for more by rejoicing over their gift. Paul

---

[2]Fowl, p. 192.
[3]Fowl, p. 194.
[4]Bockmuehl, p. 260.

has already learned (*emathon*) to be content (*autarkes*) in whatever circumstances he finds himself. He flourishes in any and every situation because he has the strength to do so by the power of Christ Jesus. It is important to state here that this contented attitude of Paul towards material things was not new, for the Stoics and Cynic philosophers exhibited a similar attitude of being independent and self-sufficient from material possessions. However, the Stoics and Cynics derived their attitude from their own power and self-discipline. Their self-sufficiency came from self-denial or detaching themselves from that thing. By contrast, Paul's power to be self-sufficient or content, and to see material support as a matter of indifference, came from Christ Jesus and was not sourced in his own self-denial.[5] Through the power Christ gave him, he had learned how to be content in times of want as well as in times of plenty. He is not saying, however, that he can do everything, as is sometimes thought. Rather, he is talking here of personal needs, which can lead to being dependent on people. Through Christ's power at work in him he has learned to be content with little or nothing by way of material possessions. Equally, he has learned how to handle plenty and not be swept away by wealth.[6]

---

[5]Bockmuehl, pp. 260f; Fowl, p.194, citing Seneca, De Vita Beata 6.2, "The happy man is content with his present lot, no matter what it is, and is reconciled to his circumstances." For them to be reconciled to one's circumstances depends on the recognition that one can do little to alter those circumstances and as such, one has only the option of mastering such circumstances and becoming indifferent to them as a way out. This, as has been said, is far removed from Paul's position.

[6]Bockmuehl, pp. 261f.

You have done well for sharing in my suffering vv. 14 - 16.

Having explained to them that his joy over their resumption of concern does not mean that he is asking for more, in vv. 14 – 16 Paul returns again to the thanksgiving he commenced in v. 10. In v. 14, he says, "Nevertheless, you have done well, having shared with me in my suffering." By using "nevertheless" he makes it clear that his explanation in vv. 11-13 does not mean a lack of gratitude for the gift. Rather they have done a good job by sharing in his suffering and in the gospel through sending him this gift. This in itself is an expression of thanks. This is more so when he reminds them that in the beginning of his preaching when he came to Macedonia, no church shared with him in material possession except they, the Philippians. They twice sent support to him when he was in Thessalonica. Paul cannot express his gratitude more strongly than reminding his supporters how much they had been giving in the past, and that only unavoidable circumstances had prevented this relationship continuing, until now.

In v. 17, he goes on to set out the benefits of the gift to them. It is this benefit to them that enthuses him most of all. For Paul, therefore, what interests him most about the gift is that their accounts in heaven have been credited. This is not surprising in such a close relationship. More so, he had said in 2: 1 - 4 that they should seek after the interests of another instead of individual personal interest, just as Jesus Christ sought our interests rather than his own. Hence, he is more excited about what the gift has yielded for them in heaven than its material benefit to him now. Nevertheless, in v. 18, he returns to expressing deep words of appreciation for the gift sent to him and for its high value. It is indeed, "a fragrant offering, an acceptable sacrifice, very pleasing to God." Again, he goes on to say that it was not given or offered to him but to God and for this, he says, God has credited it to them in their heavenly bank accounts. This again is his way of giving thanks in the highest degree. Its value is not so much what is given for the benefit of the receiver but what such giving yields to the giver. The gift expresses how much the receiver loves and how much he longed the best for the giver. This is what a deep appreciation does.

This way of expressing appreciation is understandable to an African. It is common among the Mupun of Plateau State in Nigeria to hear someone gives thanks for what is given but not necessarily expressing the very words, "Thank you very much" that is, *plang ɗes*, but he or she would say something which expresses the appreciation much more deeply than the mere, thank you like, *an vithong. Dang an a ki mi fen pe shin ha ɗakih? Dang a wurDa Naan ɗe a ɗengsi le ɗeret bwa ha ɗak oh* (And you give this even to one like me? What have I to give you? Only the Lord God who is in heaven will pay you back and bless you." This is a mixture of thanksgiving and a prayer to God to bless and reward the giver, as Paul is doing in vv. 18 and 19.

In v. 19 Paul closes the subject with a word of prayer: "And my God will fill every need of yours according to his riches in glory in Christ Jesus." Here, Paul prays that God, out of his abundant riches would supply every need of theirs in Christ Jesus. This will not be on the grounds of any good done on their part but because of the grace of Jesus Christ. This is followed by a doxology, "And to my God and Father be glory forever and ever. Amen." Just as Paul had needs to be supplied by them, so the Philippians also have spiritual and material needs, which he feels only God can meet. God is the one who has the store of innumerable riches that he gives out freely through Christ Jesus. In this way, Paul has not simply received and given thanks, but he has done this through teaching and prayer on what giving and receiving entail for the Christian. The thanksgiving expressed is a necessity because it builds the morale of the giver. The contentment expressed by the receiver is also a mark of saying thank you to God and those who give. Thus, the repayment for the good done need not be in the cash or material things normal in Greco-Roman customs, but can be rendered by prayer for the giver and wishing the giver well. This is another way of saying thank you at the highest level. Hence, the idea of reciprocity is at play here because the Philippians have given and he has received and he is equally giving back, not in cash, but in prayer to God, the supreme Giver of all things. He alone gives abundantly, filling every person according to their needs, far in excess of what they have given. This is what gladdens the heart of Paul and of any true believer. With this understanding of giving and receiving, there can be no superior and inferior feeling on either side. The giver does not expect any loyalty as recompense from the receiver, apart from the verbal thanksgiving and the receiver's prayer to God for more blessings to be poured out on the giver, because he is investing in his heavenly account. In such an understanding of giving and receiving, no one owes the other repayment and no one is superior or inferior to the other as each has given and received from the other.

This kind of mutual relationship is expressed in much more detail in 2 Corinthians 8-9. What is new here in the Philippians letter is the attitude of the receiver to what is given. The receiver need not feel inferior, because he or she can do without the gift, if he or she has learned to abound in want and in plenty because of the power that Christ offers the believer. The giver on the other hand, needs not feel superior over the receiver because he or she is actually investing in his heavenly account by giving to an individual, a church or an organization in need, not merely giving to that individual or church in need. Secondly, the giver, through his or her donations is contributing his or her share in the gospel, which again is credited to his or her heavenly account. By receiving, the receiver is doing the giver a favour, by enlarging the giver's heavenly account, as well as giving the giver the opportunity to share in the gospel of Jesus Christ. That is why the giver must not brag over his giving, because if the receiver who trusts God for his own provisions and has learned to live in plenty and in want refuses to receive, the giver has no reward.

For giving and receiving that has no room for bragging and inferiority, to take place, a deep sense of partnership must be evident, a partnership that is rooted in first giving of self to God and the leadership of the church. When this is evident, those who give, do not give to manipulate or exploit the needy or brag or look down on others. Instead they seek to share in the poverty of the other and those who receive, receive not so much because they really are in need, but because they want it to be credited to the giver and to enter into partnership with the giver, as Paul does with the Philippian Christians.

Hence Paul's unwillingness to accept support from the Corinthians, but willing acceptance of support from the Philippians. Where the giver or givers primarily gave themselves to God and to the people they gave like the Philippians and other Macedonian churches (2 Cor. 8: 5), that is they give willingly and generously without strings attached. In that context, Paul will accept their gifts joyfully and prayerfully, sharing in their plenty without feeling obliged to pay back in loyalty or otherwise. Paul teaches us that we are not supposed to accept every donation, ruling out gifts that are meant to woo the receiver to the giver's side, or to enslave the receiver or to stop the receiver from speaking freely and justly. Paul, therefore, in 2 Corinthians 9 asks the Corinthians to give willingly and generously because such giving he says, yields great returns from both God and the receiver(s). Like Paul, Seneca, a contemporary of Paul, moralist and Stoic philosopher, not only encouraged giving but also stressed giving willingly and not giving for personal aggrandizements, saying:

> Those benefits win no thanks, which though they seem great from their substance and show, are either forced from the giver or are carelessly dropped, and that comes much more gratefully which is given by a willing rather than by a full hand. The benefit which one man bestowed on me is small, but he was not able to give more; that which another gave me is great, but he hesitated, he put it off, he grumbled when he gave it, he gave it haughtily, he published it abroad, and the person he tried to please was not the one on whom he bestowed his gift - he made an offering, not to me but to his pride.[7]

Based on both what Paul and Seneca are saying, since giving is meant to create friendship and partnership and not to divide a people, the spirit and goal of giving must show this close tie of friendship. It cannot be like the giving in the club of the haves and have-nots, the superior and inferior, where the giver loads it on the receiver or the receiver is obliged to give undue loyalty to the giver. Giving is meant to cement the gap between those who have and those who do not have, between preachers and members, without placing the giver at an advantage over the receiver. This is what motivated Paul to encourage the Corinthians to join in the relief project for the Jerusalem church that was stricken by famine. The Gentile Christians have received spiritual food from the Jerusalem Christians at their time of need. On this, John Ziesler says:

> Paul's preoccupation with the collection (Greek *koinonia*, "participation") was largely because it aimed to weld together the different parts of the church, and even perhaps to symbolize the ingathering of the Gentiles. Yet the collection also had a more straightforward purpose: it aimed to ensure that the

---

[7]Seneca, Moral Essays III (On Benefits), 1: 7 2-3.

> resources of one part of the church were available for the whole
> church, especially for the poor.[8]

Churches and church leaders today would do well to follow Paul's example and understanding of giving and receiving so as to free the church and themselves from any strings attached to giving by the rich in the church and by governments. Only by emulating Paul in contentment and determination to learn to flourish in plenty and in want, will the church freely, steadfastly and successfully preach the gospel in this generation of exploitation and looking for political supporters with bags of money. To show they are free, churches and church leaders must insist on knowing the sources of money offered the church by the rich and by governments. They must have the courage to reject money that has been stolen from government and private organizations or companies. Such freedom is also to be seen in the churches ensuring that they are not dependent on government funds to run church programmes.

Churches should realise that that some of the donations they receive from rich individuals or governments is not so much because they love the church but because such governments officials or rich individuals want to buy total control or loyalty or votes of the churches. Churches that do not realise this become fertile grounds for political manipulation. Either some church leaders do not realise this or they realise but have not learned contentment and have not come to learn the power to abound in plenty and in want. They feel they must always

---

[8]J. Ziesler, (1983), p. 126, citing 2 Cor. 8: 1 - 4; 9; Gal. 2: 10; Rom. 15: 25 - 27. J. P. Sampley, (1980), p. 36, speaking on the collection for Jerusalem and the Jerusalem Council (Gal. 2: 1 - 10) says, "The collection delivered and accepted, would symbolize the unity of all the Christians they (James, Cephas, John and Paul and Barnabas) represented". G. Kittel, "Logeia" TDNT 4 (1967), p. 283 n 12; H. Conelmann, (1975), p. 295; G. D. Fee, (1987), p. 812.

have money to champion the cause of the gospel and to enable them, as leaders, stay fit for the preaching of the gospel. As a result, the church has often been dragged into undue loyalty and silence while its external and internal enemies have their reins over the church unchecked.

Apart from the strings attached to gifts given to the church and church leaders, church leaders do not always realize that their dependence on the rich, and on members of their churches who hold political office, puts a lot of undue pressure on them. To maintain their positions in the church and society some of them go to the extent of stealing money to please the church. Political office holders feel they need to donate to church projects in order to gain the church's support. Not having enough funds of their own, they steal it from the government. The Holy Bible makes it very clear that anyone who makes a believer to fall is worthy of having a millstone tied round his neck before being thrown into the sea.

The church can avoid this trap if like Paul, it cultivates the spirit of contentment like Paul and acknowledges that the church and her leaders live, not just by food and material possessions, but especially by staying true to the word of God. Church leaders and members need to come to terms with the truth of what Jesus says on the temptation to food and other material needs. Like the apostle Paul, members and church leaders must learn to be content with whatever they have, thus, "the secret of being well-fed and of going hungry, of having plenty and of being in need" without losing our balance either way (Phil. 4: 11f). This means that the prosperity gospel which teaches that financial and material blessings or wealth and security is always the will of God for all God's people are out of tune with biblical teaching.

Questions for Further Reflection and Study

1. What does giving to those in need mean to you in your culture and in what way is it related to Christian giving?
2. Why is it necessary to give for church work and to fellow Christians in need whether near and far?
3. Is giving and receiving a Christian or not a Christian thing to do?
4. What is important about thanking those who have given something to us or help us achieve a task?
5. In what ways are our giving to other people service to God and how can we improve on giving to others?

CLOSING GREETINGS, 4: 21 - 23

[21]Greet all the saints in Christ Jesus. The brethren with me do greet you. [22]All the saints greet you, especially those from the house of Caesar. [23]The grace of the Lord Jesus Christ be with your spirit.

Evidence of good relationships are seen in the network of communications including the types of greetings exchanged between the persons concerned, This is as true in the current African setting as it was in Biblical times in the Middle East. It is also true of Paul and the Christians in Philippi and in all the other churches he founded. We see the good relationship existing between Paul and the Philippians expressed in the closing greetings of the letter in vv. 21-23.

Even today greetings, whether by letter, word of mouth and through face-to-face contact are very important in cementing relationships. Some scholars often take this very lightly in the study of biblical letters. This leads to a misunderstanding of the central purpose of a letter since the opening address and the closing greetings often sum up the purpose of the letter. The closing greeting in the letter is a mark of solidarity and intimacy that shows the network of relationships existing between the writer(s), reader(s), other church workers and other churches or individuals known to both writer(s) and reader(s) in the early church. There can be no true partnership in Christ without a good and cordial network of relationships existing between individual believers and church denominations and organizations. These greetings therefore leave us in no doubt about the critical importance of partnership with one another in the gospel of Jesus Christ and with Paul and other churches elsewhere.

Thus, Paul greets all of the Philippian saints, not distinguishing between them. By saying, "greet every saint in Christ Jesus," it is not clear whether he is actually doing the greeting or he is asking someone in the church to do it on his behalf, or he is asking the saints to greet each other in Christ Jesus. Scholars disagree on who is being asked to make the greeting. Since the letter is supposed to be read aloud in the hearing of all the members of the church, it would appear that Paul is saying they should each greet one another in Christ Jesus rather than have someone to do this. This also resolves the other problem of whether "in Christ Jesus" is with reference to "every saint" or the greeting itself. In "Christ Jesus" would fit better with "Greet" than with "saint." In other words, they are to greet one another in Christ Jesus or out of reverence for Christ Jesus. However, as Fowl, says, "It is probably just as well to let the phrase point in both directions."[1] Paul then, as usual, relates the greetings of the few co-workers who were with him in prison (2: 20 - 21), whom he refers to as "the brethren who are with me." Who they are by name, Paul does not say. This is followed by relating to the Philippians the greetings of "all the saints, especially those of the house of Caesar," "All the saints" refers to the church in Rome and possibly elsewhere. Moreover, "those of the house of Caesar" would not refer to Caesar's family or relations, but to the workers in the palace who had come to believe Paul was in prison, not as a criminal, but for his faith. These would be "the civil servants (the

---

[1]See also Bockmuehl p. 268; Beare, p. 157.

slave/servants) in the imperial service" who have become used to Paul because of his testimony and way of life.[2]

What Paul does not do in this letter is to ask the Philippians to greet some known individuals in the church in Philippi, as he does in some of his other letters like, 2 Tim 3: 19, Titus 3: 15b and 1 Cor. 16: 20. Neither does he mention the names of the people who send their greetings from his side as he does in some of his other letters like Romans (16:21-24) and Colossians 4: 10-14. Nor does he mention names in his greetings to the churches in Corinth and Thessalonica. The lack of any mention of names may be for the simple reason that he has treated the Philippians as a single united body. He would not handpick some people in the church in Philippi to be specifically greeted, as he does in Romans for example. For the same reason he would not send the greetings of only a selected few among his co-workers with him, but all of them.

The benediction in v. 23 ends the letter, as in his other letters: "The grace of the Lord Jesus Christ be with your spirit." Again, as we noted with Paul's greeting in the opening address, this is as found in Greco-Roman letter closing greetings. At the same time, as with the opening address and greetings, the closing greeting in Paul's letters is also distinct from the Greco-Roman closing greetings, as it is here. Whereas in Greco-Roman letters, the closing is simply, "farewell" (Greek: *eroso*), here in Paul, it is, "The grace of the Lord Jesus Christ be with your spirit."

Thus, the letter started with wishing them peace and grace from God our Father and the Lord Jesus Christ. The grace that kept the church, despite suffering at the hands of opponents from without (1: 27 - 2: 30) and within (3: 1 - 4: 9), has made it possible for them to share in the gospel with Paul and in his wants. It is only right that

---

[2]Fowl, p. 202; Bockmuehl, p. 269.

he now closes the letter with the same wish; the grace of Jesus Christ that he wishes to be with their spirit, as they steadfastly strive together with one mind and spirit (1: 28) Thus, "your spirit" not "your spirits" here refers to their common disposition or mind-set For Bockmuehl, "the implication may be that God's grace is to be with their individual spirits as united in the fellowship of Christ."[3] Thus, his goal is to stress the communal spirit, something the church should walk in or live by, without which they can easily be intimidated by both internal and external opponents. In this way, his closing greeting and benediction fit in with his address and thanksgiving (introduction) and the body of the letter.

Questions for Further Reflection and Study

1. Discuss the nature and functions of greetings among your people and how this fits in with greetings in Paul's letters.
2. What would you say is the theology of greetings and how can this be encouraged?
3. What is the place of greetings in today's letter writing and how can we improve on it?
4. How is Paul's greeting in Philippians different from the others and why?
5. What do we learn from Paul's greetings this letter to the Philippians?

---

[3]Ibid., p. 271.

BIBLIOGRAPHY

Abate, Ashetu, "Philippians Commentary" in *Africa Bible Commentary*, Grand Rapids: Zondervan, 2006.

Berry Ken L. 'The Function of Ffriendship L anguage in Philippians 4.10-2' In *Frien♦ship, Flattery an♦ Frankness of Speech: Stu♦ies on Frien♦ship in the New Testament Worl♦*, pp. 107-24. Ed. J. T. Fitzgerald. NovTSup 82. Leiden: Brill.

Boyarin, Daniel, *A Ra♦ical Jew: Paul an♦ the Politics of I♦entity*, Berkeley: University of California Press, 1994.

Blomquist,, L. Gregory, "The Function of Suffering in Philippians" (*JSNT* Sup 78; Sheffield: Sheffield Academic Press, 1993).

Bockmuehl, Markus, *The Epistle to the Philippians*, Black's New Testament Commentary, London: Hendrickson Publishers, 1998.

Bruce, Gary M. & Lynn Cohick, Gene L Green, 2009. *The New Testament in Antiquity: A Survey of the New Testament within its cultural context*, Grand Rapids Michigan: Zondervan.

Buell, Demse Kimber, *Why This New Race, Ethnic Reasoning in Early Christianity*, New York: Columbia University Press, 2005.

Campbell, Constantine R., *Paul an♦ Union With Christ: An Exegetical an♦ Theological Stu♦y*, Grand Rapids: Zondervan, 2012.

Castelli, Elizabeth A. *Imitating Paul: A Discourse of Power*, Louisville: Westminster John Knox, 1991.

Classen, Carl Joachim, *Rhetorical Criticism of the New Testament*, Boston: Brill Academic Publisher, 2002.

Cohick, Lynn H., *The Story of God Bible Commentary: Philippians*, Grand Rapids: Zondervan, 2013.

Dahl, Nils Alstrup, "Euodia and Syntyche and Paul's Letter to the Philippians" in *The Social World of the First Christians: Essays in Honor of Wayne A. Meeks*, 3-15. Eds L. M. White & Co. Minneapolis: Fortress, 1995.

DeSilva, David A., "The Epistle to the Philippians:Uninity in the face of adversity" in *An Introduction to the New Testament: Contexts, Methods, and Ministry Formations*, Notingham: Apollos, 2004.

De Vos, Craig S., *Church and Community: The Relationship of Thessalonians, Corinthians and Philippian Churches with their wider civic communities*, Atlanta: Scholars, 1999.

Dormeyer, Detlev, *The New Testament Among the Writings of Antiquity*, Biblical Seminar 55, Sheffield: Sheffield Academic Press, 1993.

Fee, Gordon D. *Paul's Letter to the Philippians*, NICNT. Grand Rapids: Eerdmans, 1995.

Fee, G. D. *Philippians*, Leicester, England: Intervarsity Press, 1999.

Fiorenza, Elizabeth Schussler, *Rhetoric and Ethic: The Politics of Biblical Studies*, Minneapolis: Fortress Press, 1999.

Horsley, Richard A., Ed., *Paul and Empire: Religion and Power in Roman Imperial Society,* Harrisburg, Pennsylvania: Trinity Press International, 1997.

Jeffers, James S., *The Greco-Roman World of the New Testament: Exploring the Background of Early Christianity*, Downers Grove, Illinois: Inter-Varsity Press, 1999.

Klauck, Hans-Joseph, *Ancient Letters and the New Testament: A Guide to Context and Exegesis*, Waco, Texas: Baylor University Press, 2006.

Lyall, Francis, Slaves, Citizen, Sons: *Legal Metaphors in the Epistles*, Grand Rapids: Zondervan, 1987.

Peterman, G. W. "Paul's Gifts from Philippi: Conventions of Gifts Exchange and Christian Giving," *Society for New Testament Monograph Series* 92, Cambridge: Cambridge Uni Press, 1997.

Fowl, Stephen E., *Philippians*, Grand Rapids: Wm. B. Eerdman's Publishing Co., 2005.

Garland, David E. "Philippians" in *The Expositor's Bible Commentary*, Revised Edition Vol. 12: *Ephesians to Philemon* (General Eds. Tremper Longman III and David E Garland), Grand Rapids: Zondervan, 2006.

Geoffrion Timothy C., *The Rhetorical Purpose and the Political and Military Character of Philippians*: Lewiston, NY: Edwin Mellen Press, 1993.

Hansen, G. Walter, *The Letter to the Philippians,* Pillar New Testament
   Commentary, Nottingham: Apollos, 2009.

Hawthorne, Gerald F. *Philippians.* WBC 43. Waco: Word, 1983.

Oakes, Peter S. *From People to Letter,* Society for New Testament Studies
   Monograph Series, Peabody, Mass: Hendrickson, 1991.

O'Brien, Peter T., *The Epistle to the Philippians: A Commentary on the Greek Text,* The
   New International Greek Testament Commentary (NIGTC), Grand Rapids:
   William B. Eerdmans Publishing Company, 1991.

Marshall, Howard, *The Epistle to the Philippians,* London: Epworth Press, 1992.

Marchal, Joseph A., *Hierarchy, Unity, and Imitation: A Feminist Rhetorical Analysis
   of Power Dynamics in Paul's Letter to the Philippians,* Atlanta: Society of Biblical
   Literature, 2006.

Marshall, Peter, *Enmity in Corinth: Social Conventions in Paul's Relations with the
   Corinthians,* Tubingen: Mohr, 1987.

Martin, Dale B., *The Corinthian Body,* New Haven: Yale University Press, 1995.

Moo, Douglas J. & Co., "Philippians" in *An Introduction to the New Testament,*
   Notingham: Apollos, 2005.

Moulton, Harold K. (Ed.), *The Analytical Greek Lexicon Revised,* Grand Rapids:
   Zondervan, 1977.

Muller, Jac. J. *The The Epistle of Paul to the Philippians: The English Text with Introduction and Notes,* New International Commentary on the New Testament, Vol 11, Grand Rapids: William B. Eerdmans Publishing Company, 1984.

O'Brien, "Introductory Thanksgiving in the Letters of Paul." *NovTSup 49.* Leiden: Brill, 1977.

Osiek, Carolyn, 'Philippians' In *Searching the Scriptures, Vol. 2: A Feminist Theology Commentary,* 237-49. Ed E. Schussler Florenza. London: SCM, 1995.

Peterlin, Davorin, *Paul's Letters to the Philippians in the Light of Disunity in the Church, Supplements to Novum Testamentum* 79 Leiden: Brill 1995.

Peterman, G. W., *Paul's Gift From Philippi* (SNTSMS 92; Cambridge: Cambridge Univ. Press, 1997).

__________*Paul's Gift from Philippi: Conventions of Gift Exchange and Christian Giving.* Society for New Testament Monograph Series 92. Cambridge: Cambridge Univ. Press, 1997.

Portefaix, Lilian, *Rejoice Sisters: Pauls' Letters to the Philippians and Luke-Acts as received by First Century Women* (ConBNT 20; Stockholm: Almsqvist & Wikell 1988.

Richards, E. Randolph, *The Secretary in the Letters of Paul,* WUNT 2:42. Tubingen: Mohr (Siebeck), 1991.

Segovia, Fernando F. & Sugirtharajab, R. S. Eds. *A Postcolonial Commentary on the New Testament Writings,* New York/London: T & T Clark, 2009.

Silva, Moses, *The Wycliffe Exegetical Commentary: Philippians*, Chicago: Moody
Press, 1988.

Stowers, S. K., *Letter Writing in Greco-Roman Antiquity*. LEC 5. Philadelphia:
Westminster, 1986.

Swift, Robert C., "The Theme and Structure of Philippians" in *Vital New Testament
Issues: Examining New Testament Passages and Problems* (Zuck, Roy B. (Ed.),
Grand Rapids; Kregel Resources (1996) pp. 171-187.

Watson, D. F. "A Rhetorical Analysis of Philippians and its implications for the
Unity Question", *NovT* 30, pp. 59-60, (1988).